CHRIST IS RISEN!

HE HAS RISEN INDEED!

Christos Anesti!

Alithos Anesti!

Christ is Risen!
He has Risen Indeed!
Christos Anesti! Alithos Anesti!

Vinu V Das

Tabor Press

ISBN 978-1-997541-16-5

Table of Contents

Chapter 1: Foreshadowed Victory—Resurrection in the Old Testament

The theme of resurrection is woven throughout the tapestry of Scripture long before the dawn of Easter morning. In the Old Testament, hints of a coming victory over death emerge in prophetic utterances, poetic songs, and vivid narrative types. Through shadows and symbols, God prepares His people to recognize the Messiah's triumph over the grave. These early anticipations of new life underscore the unity of God's redemptive plan from Eden to the empty tomb. Even as Israel faced exile, oppression, and despair, divine promises kindled hope in a future restoration. By examining key passages—ranging from the Suffering Servant in Isaiah to the Valley of Dry Bones in Ezekiel—we discover how the Old Testament testifies to the resurrection event. This chapter explores the manifold ways in which God foreshadowed Christ's rising, demonstrating that the Easter miracle was neither unexpected nor unprecedented but rather the climactic fulfillment of ancient revelations.

1.1 Messianic Prophecies of Suffering and Triumph

The prophetic books of Israel are rich with allusions to a coming Deliverer who would suffer on behalf of His people and then enter into glory. Messianic prophecies in Isaiah, Psalms, and Zechariah speak not only of sorrow and sacrifice but also of vindication and victory beyond the grave. These texts paint a portrait of One who bears infirmities, endures rejection, and is counted among transgressors—yet whose life and ministry are ultimately validated by God's vindicating power. By contrasting the humiliation of the Servant with the exaltation that follows, the prophets reveal a two-fold pattern: suffering followed by triumph. Such patterns were preserved in the collective memory of Israel, shaping expectations of divine intervention. Even though many of these prophecies appeared mysterious or even paradoxical, they set the stage for understanding Christ's passion and resurrection. Hence, the New Testament writers draw heavily on these Old Testament passages to interpret Jesus' death and rising as the fulfillment of Scripture.

1.1.1 The Suffering Servant (Isaiah 52–53)

Isaiah chapters 52 and 53 present one of the most poignant portraits of the Messiah as the Suffering Servant. In these passages, the Servant is described as "despised and rejected by men" (Isaiah 53:3) and as one who "bore our griefs and carried our sorrows" (Isaiah 53:4). The text goes on to declare that "with his wounds we are healed" (Isaiah 53:5), alluding to a substitutionary atonement that anticipates Christ's crucifixion. Remarkably, the narrative shifts from suffering to exaltation: "Therefore I will divide him a portion with the many, and he shall divide the spoil with the strong" (Isaiah 53:12). This movement from degradation to glory foreshadows the resurrection, highlighting that the Servant's mission concludes not with defeat but with divine vindication. Early Christians embraced this prophecy when they proclaimed Jesus' death and resurrection as its fulfillment (Acts 8:32–35). Isaiah's vivid language both assures believers that Messiah's pain was purposeful and affirms God's ultimate triumph over sin and death.

1.1.2 "You Will Not Abandon My Soul" (Psalm 16:8–11)

In Psalm 16, David expresses unshakable confidence that God will preserve his life: "For you will not abandon my soul to Sheol, or let your holy one see corruption" (Psalm 16:10). Although penned centuries before Christ, this verse finds its ultimate realization in the resurrection, for Christ's body did not undergo decay (Acts 13:35–37). The psalmist's declaration that "you make known to me the path of life; in your presence there is fullness of joy; at your right hand are pleasures forevermore" (Psalm 16:11) underscores the blessed hope rooted in divine deliverance. Early New Testament writers cite this psalm when explaining that Jesus' rising on the third day was not a divine surprise but the necessary fulfillment of David's prophecy (Acts 2:25–32). In this way, Psalm 16 bridges the experiences of David with those of the Messiah, assuring readers that God's faithfulness extends from the human king to the eternal King.

1.1.3 "The Pierced Shepherd" (Zechariah 12:10)

Zechariah 12:10 foretells that God will "pour out on the house of David and the inhabitants of Jerusalem a spirit of grace and pleas for mercy," and "they will look on me, whom they have pierced." This piercing evokes imagery of crucifixion, though the prophet describes a future moment of realization and repentance. The piercing is not the end of the story; rather, it becomes the catalyst for a communal awakening: grief turns to faith as the people recognize the significance of the One they pierced. The ensuing tide of repentance paves the way for restoration and blessing. When readers view Zechariah's words through the lens of Christ's death and resurrection, the prophecy acquires new resonance: piercing leads to restoration, death to life. Thus, Zechariah's vision functions as a prophetic precursor to Easter, anticipating a reversal of despair through divine grace.

1.2 Shadows and Types of New Life

Scripture often employs historical narratives as types or shadows that prefigure later realities in Christ. These narrative types hint at resurrection by illustrating themes such as deliverance from death, divine reversal of human calamity, and new beginnings emerging from desperation. Jonah's emergence from the fish, Joseph's ascent from the pit, and the institution of the Passover lamb all function as instructive templates. Each account offers a partial glimpse into the power that God ultimately unleashes in the resurrection of Christ. While none of these shadows fully encapsulates the resurrection event, they collectively train the faithful to recognize God's capacity to overturn death, condemn despair, and inaugurate a new covenant era. By exploring these types, believers gain deeper appreciation for how the Old Testament story line culminates in the life, death, and rising of Jesus.

1.2.1 Jonah's Three-Day Deliverance (Jonah 1–2)

Jonah's ordeal in the belly of the great fish provides one of the most vivid prefigurations of burial and rising. After fleeing God's commission, Jonah ends up swallowed by a "great fish" where he spends "three days and three nights" (Jonah 1:17). In that confined space, Jonah cries out to the Lord in prayer, acknowledging God's saving power (Jonah 2:1–9). His subsequent expulsion onto dry land functions as a form of resurrection: God delivers him from certain death and grants him renewed mission. Jesus Himself invokes Jonah's experience when foretelling His own death and resurrection, saying, "For just as Jonah was three days and three nights in the belly of the great fish, so will the Son of Man be three days and three nights in the heart of the earth" (Matthew 12:40). Thus, Jonah's experience serves not merely as an isolated miracle but as a typological sign pointing to the greater deliverance in Christ.

1.2.2 Joseph's Rise from the Pit (Genesis 37; 40–41)

Joseph's dramatic ascent—from a pit of betrayal to the pinnacle of power in Egypt—reflects the motif of reversal central to resurrection. Sold as a slave by his brothers and cast into a pit (Genesis 37:23–24), Joseph later finds himself unjustly imprisoned (Genesis 39:20). Yet God elevates him: from prison to Pharaoh's court, he becomes a savior of nations during famine (Genesis 41:41–43). Although Joseph's story does not include physical resurrection, it foreshadows the life-giving reversal at the heart of Easter: disgrace transformed into glory, despair reversed into hope. His deliverance underscores God's ability to redeem dire circumstances and preaches a lesson about God's sovereignty over life's lows and highs. By reading Joseph's narrative as a type, believers discern an early affirmation that God can and will bring good from apparent ruin.

1.2.3 The Passover Lamb: From Death to New Beginning (Exodus 12)

The institution of the Passover marks a seminal moment in Israel's history: by the blood of a spotless lamb on their doorposts, the firstborn are spared from death (Exodus 12:7–13). This event prefigures Christ's sacrificial death, for He is the "Lamb of God who takes away the sin of the world" (John 1:29). As the Israelites were delivered from physical bondage, so believers find deliverance from spiritual death through Christ's atoning work. The Passover ritual pointed forward to the Last Supper, where Jesus said, "This is my body, which is given for you. Do this in remembrance of me" (Luke 22:19). In this way, the Passover lamb becomes a shadow of the true Lamb whose death inaugurates eternal life. The type emphasizes that redemption through sacrificial blood is foundational to understanding resurrection power.

1.2.4 Isaac's Binding and God's Gift of Life (Genesis 22)

In Genesis 22, Abraham's obedience is tested by God's command to offer his son Isaac as a sacrifice. At the moment of crisis, God intervenes, providing a ram in place of Isaac (Genesis 22:13). While Isaac is not literally killed and resurrected, the narrative conveys a dramatic rescue that foreshadows God's provision of life instead of death. Hebrews 11:17–19 interprets Abraham's faith as believing "that God was able even to raise him from the dead," envisioning a resurrection beyond the type itself. The binding and deliverance of Isaac thus become theological pointers toward faith in resurrection hope. Through this story, readers grasp that God's design for sacrifice is inseparable from His power to preserve and restore life.

1.3 Poetic Visions of Restoration

Wisdom literature and poetic psalms often contemplate the themes of suffering, death, and ultimate vindication. The poets of Israel grapple with anguish in vivid language yet interweave strands of hope that anticipate a reality beyond death. Poems like Psalm 22, Psalm 30, and Psalm 71 articulate confidence that God hears cries of distress and will one day deliver from the grave's grip. Likewise, Job's affirmation "I know that my Redeemer lives" (Job 19:25) rises from the depths of suffering to a triumphant declaration. Proverbs personifies Wisdom as present at creation's dawn (Proverbs 8:22–31), hinting at a cosmic order that cannot be overturned by decay. These poetic visions saturate the reader with expectancy— expectancy that is ultimately fulfilled in Christ's resurrection. By dwelling on these passages, believers gain a richer sense of the emotional and theological contours of resurrection hope.

1.3.1 Psalms of Resurrection Hope (Psalm 22; 30; 71)

Psalm 22 begins with the anguished cry, "My God, my God, why have you forsaken me?" (Psalm 22:1), only to ascend to praise as the psalmist anticipates life restored (Psalm 22:25–31). Likewise, Psalm 30 recounts a personal rescue from death: "You have turned for me my mourning into dancing; you have loosed my sackcloth and clothed me with gladness" (Psalm 30:11). Psalm 71 pledges lifelong trust in God's justice and enduring salvation: "You are my hope and my fortress, my tower and my refuge" (Psalm 71:3). Each of these psalms transitions from lament to praise, embodying resurrection's emotional trajectory—from sorrow to joy, from fear to confident trust. The psalmists' portrayal of God as a deliverer from death resonates powerfully when read alongside Christ's rising. These poems function as both personal laments and prophetic foreshadowings, assuring believers that divine rescue transcends mortal boundaries.

1.3.2 Job's Declaration of Life Beyond the Grave (Job 19:25–27)

In the book of Job, the righteous sufferer utters one of Scripture's most poignant affirmations of resurrection: "I know that my Redeemer lives, and at the last he will stand upon the earth. And after my skin has been thus destroyed, yet in my flesh I shall see God" (Job 19:25–26). Uttered in the midst of unbearable anguish, this confession defies despair by embracing a vision of bodily restoration. Job's use of the term "Redeemer" (Hebrew: go'el) conveys the idea of a kinsman-redeemer who secures justice and life. His certainty that he will see God "in my flesh" points to resurrection, not merely spiritual survival. Although Job lived centuries before the cross, his words became a beacon of hope for a future vindication that conquers mortality. This profound testimony affirms that even in the darkest trials, God's faithfulness extends into eternity.

1.3.3 Wisdom's Song of Eternal Foundations (Proverbs 8:22–31)

Proverbs 8 portrays Wisdom as a personified agent present at creation: "The LORD possessed me at the beginning of his work, the first of his acts of old" (Proverbs 8:22). The passage exalts Wisdom as delighting in humanity (Proverbs 8:30), suggesting that the Creator's intention was for His creatures to share in an enduring relationship. By highlighting Wisdom's role in weaving cosmic order, the text intimates that death and decay are intrusions upon an originally good design. Wisdom's foundational presence implies a reality that transcends temporal limitations, laying the groundwork for believing in resurrection. While Proverbs does not explicitly mention rising from the dead, its celebration of divine order and purpose fuels confidence that God will one day restore all things. In this way, Wisdom literature complements prophetic and poetic voices, underscoring the coherence of resurrection hope across genres.

1.4 Apocalyptic Hints of Cosmic Renewal

The prophets of Israel ventured beyond immediate circumstances to envision a renewed cosmos, where lifelessness gives way to vibrant restoration. Ezekiel's vision of dry bones coming to life portrays God's power to reconstitute a scattered, defeated people. Daniel's apocalyptic visions speak of a final resurrection and the establishment of everlasting dominion by the Son of Man. These apocalyptic texts frame resurrection not merely as an isolated event but as part of a grand cosmic renewal. They connect individual hope with collective destiny, assuring God's faithful that death—and even national exile—will not thwart His ultimate purposes. By exploring these visions, readers apprehend resurrection as cosmic in scope, encompassing personal deliverance and universal restoration.

1.4.1 Valley of Dry Bones Animated (Ezekiel 37:1–14)

In Ezekiel 37, the prophet is set down in a valley full of dry bones, symbolizing Israel's national despair. God commands him to prophesy over the bones: "Behold, I will cause breath to enter you, and you shall live" (Ezekiel 37:5). As Ezekiel's words speak life, sinews, flesh, and skin cover the bones, and God breathes His Spirit into them (Ezekiel 37:7–10). The vision culminates in God's promise: "I will put my Spirit within you, and you shall live" (Ezekiel 37:14). This dramatic scene foreshadows not only Israel's political restoration from exile but also the resurrection power that reanimates dead bodies. Ezekiel's apocalyptic imagery reminds readers that salvation involves both spiritual renewal and physical life. The passage thus stands as a powerful precursor to the New Testament teaching on resurrection by the Spirit.

1.4.2 The Resurrection at the End of Days (Daniel 12:1–3)

Daniel 12 introduces a climactic resurrection at the close of history: "And many of those who sleep in the dust of the earth shall awake, some to everlasting life, and some to shame and everlasting contempt" (Daniel 12:2). This verse explicitly envisions a general resurrection—both of the righteous and the unrighteous—underscoring that bodily raising is part of God's eschatological plan. The promise that "those who are wise shall shine like the brightness of the sky above" (Daniel 12:3) highlights the vindicatory and transformative aspects of resurrection. Daniel's apocalyptic scope broadens resurrection from individual hope to cosmic judgment and reward. It assures believers that earthly sufferings yield to eternal outcomes determined by divine justice. This apocalyptic dimension deepens the believer's understanding of resurrection as integral to God's end-time purposes.

1.4.3 The Son of Man's Everlasting Dominion (Daniel 7:13–14)

In Daniel 7, the prophet beholds "one like a son of man" coming with the clouds of heaven, receiving "dominion and glory and a kingdom" that shall never be destroyed (Daniel 7:13–14). While this vision emphasizes the establishment of God's kingdom, it also implies victory over all opposing powers—including death itself. The Son of Man's authority extends to "all peoples, nations, and languages," indicating a universal reign rooted in resurrection life. By depicting cosmic redemption under the Son of Man, Daniel's prophecy foreshadows the Messiah's conquering of death and rise to sovereign rule. Early Christians recognized this imagery in Christ's resurrection and ascension (Matthew 26:64; Acts 7:56), seeing in Daniel's vision the inauguration of the new creation. Thus, Daniel's apocalyptic portrayal ties resurrection to kingly power and cosmic restoration.

1.5 Covenantal Promises of Restoration

Beyond narrative types and prophetic visions, the Old Testament contains explicit covenantal promises that anticipate a transformative renewal. Jeremiah speaks of a "new covenant" in which God writes His law on human hearts, implying a moved-from-within transformation that parallels resurrection. Amos proclaims an ingathering promise for Israel, while Hosea declares God's power to ransom from death. These covenantal assurances link God's faithfulness to future redemption, portraying restoration as both relational and corporeal. They underscore that, under the coming covenant, God's people will experience a life-changing renewal—one that culminates in resurrection. By tracing these promises, readers perceive resurrection as the divine fulfillment of relational commitments made long ago.

1.5.1 The New Covenant Written on Hearts (Jeremiah 31:31–34)

Jeremiah 31 unveils God's promise of a new covenant: "I will put my law within them, and I will write it on their hearts" (Jeremiah 31:33). This covenant differs from the Mosaic covenant on tablets of stone, for it involves transformative internal renewal. Although the text does not explicitly mention physical resurrection, the promise of inward change presumes a spiritual rebirth that transcends old limitations. By granting an experiential knowledge of God—"for they shall all know me, from the least of them to the greatest" (Jeremiah 31:34)—this covenant lays the groundwork for everlasting life with God. The New Testament identifies Jesus as the mediator of this covenant (Hebrews 8:6–13), whose death and rising inaugurate heart-level transformation and guarantee bodily resurrection. Thus, Jeremiah's promise finds its consummation in the life-giving work of Christ.

1.5.2 Exile Turned into Firstfruits (Amos 9:11–15)

Amos 9:11–15 prophesies that "the days are coming" when God will restore David's fallen tent and raise up the ruins of Israel (Amos 9:11). The passage continues: "I will plant them on their land, and they shall never again be uprooted" (Amos 9:15). While focused on national restoration, these words intimate a resurrection of fortunes—replacing desolation with flourishing life. Israel's return from exile becomes a foretaste of the broader resurrection reality. By lifting His hand and rebuilding David's fallen tent, God demonstrates creative power akin to raising the dead. New Testament writers see in

Amos's promise a parallel to the resurrection: God's final act of replanting His people into an unshakable kingdom (Acts 15:16–17). Therefore, Amos's vision contributes to the mosaic of resurrection hope by framing restoration in national and covenantal dimensions.

1.5.3 God's Faithfulness Beyond Death (Hosea 13:14)

In Hosea 13:14, God declares: "I will ransom them from the power of Sheol; I will redeem them from Death. O Death, where are your plagues? O Sheol, where is your sting?" This triumphant challenge confronts death face-to-face, forfeiting its power. Paul later echoes these words in 1 Corinthians 15:55 when celebrating Christ's victory over death through resurrection. Hosea's oracle thus provides one of the clearest Old Testament anticipations of defeating death itself. By pledging to redeem from Sheol, God assures His people that divine faithfulness perseveres even beyond the grave. This promise elevates resurrection from a miraculous wonder to a covenantal guarantee. The confrontation with death's sting signals that death is neither uncontested nor ultimate in God's purposes.

1.6 Preparing for the Risen Messiah

Having surveyed prophetic, poetic, and narrative anticipations of resurrection, we discern an Old Testament panorama in which God steadily prepares His people for the climactic event of Easter. The tapestry of shadows, promises, and visions underscores the continuity of redemptive history, revealing that Christ's rising was neither an ad-hoc wonder nor an afterthought. Rather, it stands as the culmination of divine self-revelation and covenantal faithfulness. In tracing these threads, believers recognize the unity of Scripture and the coherence of God's plan to conquer sin and death. This preparation deepens our understanding of the resurrection's significance and intensifies our worshipful response to the risen Lord.

1.6.1 Continuity of God's Redemptive Plan

From Eden's promise of a seed to crush the serpent's head (Genesis 3:15) to the apocalyptic visions of a new creation, Scripture unfolds a seamless story of redemption. Every type, prophecy, and promise in the Old Testament contributes to a cumulative anticipation of Messiah's triumph. This continuity illustrates that resurrection is not an isolated miracle but the apex of God's irreversible plan. By recognizing the theological threads connecting covenant, sacrifice, and kingdom, Christians appreciate the resurrection as the nexus of divine love and justice. Such a holistic view affirms that every moment in redemptive history—whether in the wilderness, the monarchy, or the exile—prepares the way for Easter's victory. In this light, the New Testament's affirmation of Christ's rising resonates as the fulfillment of ancient longings.

1.6.2 Old Covenant Shadows Serving the New

Ceremonial laws, sacrificial systems, and symbolic narratives of the Old Covenant function as pedagogical tools, training Israel to anticipate greater realities in Christ. The Law's rituals point to the perfect sacrifice, while the feasts foreshadow the chronology of redemption culminating in the Passover–Easter rhythm. The repeated cycle of consecration, sacrifice, and restoration shapes Israel's imagination, keeping alive the hope of divine intervention. When Jesus fulfills these shadows—bearing sin as the Passover Lamb and rising as the firstfruits—believers recognize the coherence of God's economy. The Old Covenant thus serves as a schoolmaster, guiding hearts toward the true substance realized in Christ's resurrection. Understanding these connections enhances worship and deepens appreciation for the New Covenant's novelty.

1.6.3 Anticipating the Fullness of Resurrection

As the Old Testament closes, God's people stand on the cusp of unheard-of restoration: suffering is about to yield to triumph, exile to reunion, death to life. Through the prophetic voices and narrative illustrations we have explored, Israel's faith is continually rehearsed for the moment when the Messiah will conquer the grave. New Testament authors remind us that "these things were written for our instruction" (Romans 15:4), urging readers to embrace the hope kindled by ancient texts. Today, Christians approach Easter not as a distant or obscure promise but as the realized center of redemptive history. By anticipating the fullness of resurrection, believers live in the tension between "already" and "not yet," empowered by the Spirit to bear witness to the world. Thus, the Old Testament prepares the church to proclaim with confidence: Christ is risen indeed!

Conclusion The Old Testament abounds with anticipations of resurrection, weaving together prophetic pronouncements, instructive types, poetic laments turned praise, apocalyptic visions, and covenantal assurances. Each genre contributes a unique facet to the portrait of God's ultimate victory over death, revealing a multifaceted hope that spans individual deliverance and cosmic renewal. From Isaiah's Suffering Servant to Ezekiel's Valley of Dry Bones, these ancient texts testify that the miraculous event of resurrection was never foreign to Israel's faith. Rather, it stood at the heart of God's redemptive narrative, poised to find its definitive fulfillment in Jesus Christ. As we reflect on these foreshadowings, our confidence in Easter deepens, for we see that Christ's triumph is the crowning act of a story authored by a faithful God. May this awareness not only enrich our theological understanding but also ignite renewed worship, as we live each day in the light of the risen Lord's unending victory.

Chapter 2: The Way of the Cross— From Crucifixion to Tomb

The journey from the Upper Room to the sealed tomb encompasses the heart of Christian faith: the cross and the grave. In this chapter, we trace each step of Jesus' path to death, examining how His final hours fulfill Old Testament shadows and inaugurate the New Covenant. Far from being haphazard or solely tragic, the events of the Passion unfold according to divine purpose, revealing layers of meaning in every gesture, word, and sign. From the Passover context of the Last Supper to the darkened skies over Golgotha, each moment testifies to God's redemptive plan. Jesus' voluntary submission to betrayal and judgment exposes the depth of His love, while the tearing of the temple veil and the confession of a Roman centurion affirm His cosmic significance. By attending closely to the Gospel narratives, we honor the magnitude of Christ's sacrifice and prepare our hearts to behold the miracle of Easter morning. As we journey together through trials, prayers, and tomb-side sorrow, may our faith be deepened by the rich textures of the way of the cross.

2.1 The Last Supper and the New Covenant

On the eve of His crucifixion, Jesus gathered His disciples to celebrate the Passover in an upper room, thereby linking His impending death to Israel's deliverance from Egypt. By situating the Lord's Supper within the Passover framework, He signaled that He Himself was the true Passover Lamb whose blood would bring freedom from the bondage of sin (Matthew 26:17–19; Exodus 12:1–14). In breaking the bread and sharing the cup, Jesus established a new covenant, inviting His followers to remember His body given and His blood poured out for many (Luke 22:19–20; Jeremiah 31:31–34). This ritual did more than memorialize His death; it inaugurated a perpetual ordinance through which believers participate in Christ's sacrificial work. The disciples could not yet grasp the full import of His words, but history shows that the early church treasured these instructions as foundational to communal worship (1 Corinthians 11:23–26). In the fragility of unleavened bread and the bitterness of the sour wine, Jesus embodied the paradox of death leading to life. Thus, the Last Supper stands as both farewell banquet and covenantal pledge, anchoring the cross in the rich soil of Israel's story.

2.1.1 The Passover Context

Jesus chose the time of Passover to celebrate His final meal, invoking themes of liberation and divine judgment. Each element of the Passover—unblemished lamb, blood on the doorposts, unleavened bread, and bitter herbs—pointed backward to Egypt and forward to the cross. By identifying Himself as the Lamb, Jesus claimed both the role of sacrificial victim and the sufferer who would bear the world's sin (John 1:29; 1 Corinthians 5:7). The disciples' participation in the Passover meal thus became an anticipatory act, symbolizing their inclusion in the deliverance that Christ would accomplish. In doing so, Jesus reinterpreted the ritual, transforming it from a national remembrance into a personal encounter with divine grace. The Passover's focus on remembrance ("Do this in remembrance of me") challenged believers to live in the perpetual awareness of redemption (Luke 22:19). Through this context, the Last Supper emerges not merely as a historical event but as the hinge upon which Old Covenant ceremony swings into New Covenant reality.

2.1.2 Institution of the Lord's Supper

During the meal, Jesus took bread, gave thanks, broke it, and gave it to His disciples, saying, "This is my body, which is given for you" (Luke 22:19). He then took the cup, declaring, "This cup is the new covenant in my blood, which is poured out for you" (Luke 22:20). These words establish the sacramental language that undergirds Christian worship across centuries. By linking physical elements—bread and wine—to spiritual realities—body and blood—Jesus rendered visible the invisible work of atonement. The apostle Paul later reiterates this command in 1 Corinthians, emphasizing the centrality of communion to church life (1 Corinthians 11:23–26). The participatory nature of the Supper invites believers into intimate solidarity with Christ: they eat the bread of sacrifice and drink the cup of atonement. In every generation, the Lord's Supper recalls both the cost of sin and the victory over death secured by Calvary's blood.

2.1.3 The New Covenant in Jesus' Blood

When Jesus spoke of the "new covenant," He invoked Jeremiah's prophecy that God would write His law on human hearts (Jeremiah 31:31–34). This covenant promised internal transformation rather than external regulation. By framing His blood as the covenantal seal, Jesus affirmed that His death would inaugurate a relationship grounded in divine grace, not in human effort. The writer of Hebrews expounds that Christ is the mediator of a better covenant, established on better promises (Hebrews 8:6–13). His sacrifice fulfills and surpasses the sacrificial system of the Old Covenant, rendering obsolete the repeated offerings of bulls and goats (Hebrews 10:1–18). In drinking the cup, believers symbolically receive the benefits of this covenant—pardon of sins, unity with God, and empowerment by the Spirit. Thus, the blood of Christ stands at the center of redemptive history as the locus of divine mercy and the guarantee of eternal life.

2.2 Farewell Discourses and Prayers

Following the Supper, Jesus spent His final hours imparting profound teachings and pouring out His heart in prayer. In private discourse with His disciples (John 13–17), He prepared them for the trials to come and promised the abiding presence of the Holy Spirit. His words weave together comfort, instruction, and warning, as He calls them to love, obedience, and witness. After these teachings, He withdrew to Gethsemane to wrestle in prayer, modeling perfect submission to the Father's will. The contrast between the intimacy of the farewell discourses and the agony of the garden highlights the dual reality of Sonship—glory in obedience, suffering in service. By exploring these movements of teaching and prayer, we see how deeply Jesus cared for His followers and how resolutely He committed Himself to the path of sacrifice.

2.2.1 The Farewell Discourse (John 13–17)

In the upper room, Jesus unfolds a complex tapestry of theology and exhortation. He begins with humble service, washing His disciples' feet as a parable of servant leadership (John 13:1–17). He then pronounces a "new commandment" of mutual love (John 13:34–35) and foretells His departure and return (John 14:1–4). Jesus promises the Spirit of truth, who will teach and guide them after He is gone (John 14:16–17; 16:7–15). He reassures them of peace that transcends circumstances, not as the world gives (John 14:27). In John 15, He uses the vine and branches to illustrate abiding in Him, stressing that fruitful Christian life flows from union with the true vine. Finally, Jesus prays for the unity and sanctification of His disciples, interceding for them and all who will believe (John 17:20–26). This discourse knits together promises of love, presence, and purpose, equipping the church to carry forward His mission in the world.

2.2.1.1 The New Commandment: "Love One Another"

At the heart of the farewell discourse lies the new commandment: "Love one another as I have loved you" (John

13:34). This mandate elevates Christian love above mere obligation, rooting it in the self-giving example of Christ. The measure of love is the cross itself: soldiers pierced His hands and feet (John 19:18–37), yet He laid down His life willingly. By calling love "new," Jesus signals a deeper dimension than the Old Testament command "love your neighbor as yourself" (Leviticus 19:18). His love is sacrificial, unconditional, and transformative, enabling believers to embody the reign of God in community. When the early church practiced this love publicly, it became a compelling witness to the world (Acts 2:42–47). Thus, the new commandment grounds Christian ethics in the reality of Christ's sacrificial love.

2.2.1.2 Promise of the Paraclete (Holy Spirit)

Jesus promises to send another Advocate, the Holy Spirit, to dwell with and in His disciples (John 14:16–17; 16:7–15). The Spirit's work includes convicting the world of sin, guiding into truth, and glorifying Christ. This divine Helper equips followers with wisdom, boldness, and power for mission (Acts 1:8). Unlike the temporary presence of Moses or Elijah, the Spirit's indwelling presence is permanent, sealing believers until the day of redemption (Ephesians 1:13–14). The promise of the Paraclete shifts the paradigm: no longer will God's presence be confined to a temple, but He will dwell within individual hearts. By commissioning the Spirit, Jesus assures His church that His empowering presence transcends physical absence, continuing His work through every generation.

2.2.2 Gethsemane: Agony and Submission

After conveying profound promises, Jesus withdraws with Peter, James, and John to the garden of Gethsemane, where the weight of impending suffering presses upon Him. He falls to the ground, praying that the cup of suffering might pass, yet submitting to the Father's will: "Not my will, but yours, be done" (Luke 22:42). This moment reveals the depth of His humanity—anguish, sorrow, and foreboding mingle as He anticipates betrayal and mocking. Simultaneously, the garden scene exemplifies perfect obedience: even in agony, Jesus aligns His will with the divine plan of redemption. His prayer demonstrates that true strength often comes through surrender and trust. Meanwhile, the disciples, overwhelmed by grief, fall asleep, unable to heed His command to "watch and pray" (Matthew 26:41). Their weakness contrasts with Jesus' steadfast resolve, underscoring His unique role as the obedient Son who alone could fulfill the Father's redemptive purposes.

2.2.2.1 Jesus' Prayer of Surrender

In Gethsemane, Jesus prays three times, each time returning to His companions to find them sleeping (Mark 14:32–42). His first prayer petitions for the removal of suffering—"Abba, Father, all things are possible for you; remove this cup from me" (Mark 14:36)—yet He adds, "yet not what I will, but what you will." The repetition underscores His wrestling spirit, mirroring the intensity of human prayer and struggle. In these prayers, Jesus models perfect submission: He lays His desires before the Father, acknowledges divine sovereignty, and accepts the path of obedience. Through this example, believers are taught to approach God honestly, bringing fears and hopes alike, and to trust in God's wisdom above their own. The garden thus becomes a holy school of prayer, where the cost of obedience is made visible.

2.2.2.2 The Disciples' Sleepless Vigil

While Jesus agonizes, Peter, James, and John stand at a distance, expected to watch and pray alongside Him (Matthew 26:38–39). Yet grief overtakes them, and they slumber, failing to support their Master in His hour of need. Their sleep accentuates the loneliness of Jesus' suffering and highlights human frailty in the face of divine calling. When rebuked by Jesus—"Could you not watch with me one hour?"—they awaken to the reality that spiritual vigilance is costly (Matthew 26:40–41). This contrast between divine resolve and human weakness sets the stage for the betrayal that follows, illustrating our need for grace and the perils of spiritual lethargy. In their failure, the disciples teach us about dependence on Christ's strength rather than our own.

2.3 Arrest, Trials, and Denials

As dawn approaches, the tranquility of Gethsemane gives way to violence and legal proceedings. A crowd armed with swords and clubs, led by Judas, descends upon Jesus, fulfilling ancient prophecy about betrayal (Psalm 41:9; Zechariah 13:7). He is taken first to the Jewish council (Sanhedrin), where accusations of blasphemy lead to a guilty verdict. Meanwhile, Peter denies any association with Jesus three times, fulfilling the Lord's prediction (Matthew 26:34). Jesus is then sent to Pontius Pilate, the Roman governor, and briefly to Herod Antipas, before Pilate yields to the crowd's pressure, sentencing Jesus to crucifixion. This sequence of illegal trials, false accusations, and political expediency lays bare the depth of human sin and the cost of divine love. Each stage—from betrayal to judgment—reveals a facet of Christ's kingly passion and His submission to unjust authority.

2.3.1 The Betrayal by Judas

Judas Iscariot, one of the twelve, agrees with chief priests to betray Jesus for thirty pieces of silver (Matthew 26:14–16). Under the cover of night, he leads a detachment of soldiers into Gethsemane and identifies Jesus with a kiss (Matthew 26:47–50). This act transforms an intimate symbol of friendship into a sign of treachery, intensifying the pathos of Christ's journey. Jesus addresses Judas as "Friend" (Matthew 26:50), maintaining grace even in betrayal. The silent shock among the disciples underscores the jarring reality of human unfaithfulness. In fulfilling Zechariah's prophecy, the betrayal reminds us that God can bring redemption from human sin (Zechariah 13:7). Thus, Judas's kiss becomes emblematic of the world's rejection of its Savior.

2.3.2 Trial before the Sanhedrin

Jesus is first brought before Caiaphas and the Sanhedrin, where false witnesses testify against Him (Matthew 26:59–60). The high priest demands a verdict, but the charges—blasphemy and claiming to be the Son of God—confound coherent testimony. Finally, Jesus boldly affirms His identity:

"You will see the Son of Man seated at the right hand of Power and coming on the clouds of heaven" (Mark 14:62). At this, the council renders Him guilty and sentences Him to death (Mark 14:64). The illegal nature of the night trial—absence of proper defense, collusion of witnesses—exposes the miscarriage of justice. Yet Christ's silent dignity and authoritative claim highlight His Messianic prerogatives. This confrontation sets the theological stage for the cross: God's true King condemned by His own people.

2.3.3 Peter's Threefold Denial

While Jesus endures condemnation, Peter follows at a distance, only to deny Jesus three times when questioned (Luke 22:54–62; John 18:17–27). Each denial—first to a servant girl, then to bystanders—echoes the prophecy "I will strike the shepherd, and the sheep will be scattered" (Zechariah 13:7). Peter's weeping upon realizing his failure poignantly depicts repentance and the gravity of sin. His broken heart contrasts with the shameless self-defense offered by others, illustrating the cost of fear over faith. In later encounters, Jesus restores Peter with the thrice-repeated question, "Do you love me?" (John 21:15–17). This restoration foreshadows the power of resurrection grace to mend broken relationships and commission fallen disciples for future ministry.

2.3.4 Trial before Pilate and Herod

After Jewish condemnation, Jesus is delivered to Pontius Pilate, the Roman governor, marking a shift from religious to civil jurisdiction (John 18:28–38). Though Pilate finds no guilt warranting death, he yields to the crowd's demands for crucifixion (John 19:4–16). Jesus is then sent to Herod Antipas—who likewise dismisses Him after mockery (Luke 23:6–12)—before being returned to Pilate. This back-and-forth exposes the vacillation of political power and the influence of public opinion. Ultimately, Pilate succumbs to fear of rebellion, symbolically washing his hands yet authorizing innocent blood (Matthew 27:24–26). In these trials, Jesus stands silent against falsehood, embodying the suffering Servant who opens not His mouth (Isaiah 53:7).

2.3.4.1 Pilate's Interrogation and Proclamation of Innocence

Pilate questions Jesus: "Are you the King of the Jews?" to which Jesus replies, "You say so" (Matthew 27:11). Finding no treasonous intent, Pilate declares Him innocent three times— "I find no guilt in this man" (Luke 23:4,14–15). Yet, despite his verdict, Pilate fears the crowd more than the truth, illustrating Rome's moral bankruptcy. His internal conflict—justice versus self-preservation—plays out in the courtyard as he offers to release Jesus or Barabbas, a convicted criminal (Luke 23:17). The crowd's choice of Barabbas underscores the tragic irony of preferring rebellion over redemption. Pilate's reluctant complicity fulfills prophetic imagery of God's righteous One being delivered into unjust hands.

2.3.4.2 Herod's Mockery and Return to Pilate

Hearing of Jesus' Galilean origin, Pilate sends Him to Herod Antipas, the tetrarch, who delights in seeing Jesus perform miracles (Luke 23:7–8). Expecting a spectacle, Herod questions Jesus but receives no answer, so he and his soldiers mock Him—dressing Him in a robe and sending Him back (Luke 23:9–11). This farcical trial highlights the absurdity of worldly power confronted with divine silence. Herod's disdainful amusement contrasts sharply with Jesus' serenity in the face of humiliation. By returning Him to Pilate, Herod unwittingly advances the divine script: Jesus is handed from one authority to another, each incapable of thwarting the Father's will. The encounter foreshadows the cosmic courtroom where God alone ultimately judges.

2.3.4.3 The Crowd Chooses Barabbas

Pilate offers the Passover custom of releasing a prisoner, expecting the crowd to choose Jesus, but they demand Barabbas instead (Mark 15:6–15). Barabbas, a rebel and murderer, represents the very lawlessness Jesus came to atone for. The crowd's choice reveals human preference for immediate gratification and sensationalism over sacrificial love and justice. Pilate's attempts to reason with the masses fail, as their shouts grow louder—and more damning— "Crucify him!" (Matthew 27:22–23). In this moment, the sovereign God uses the free will of sinners to accomplish the redemptive plan, offering life in death. The choice of Barabbas encapsulates the Gospel paradox: Christ dies so that rebels may go free.

2.4 The Road to Calvary

Condemned to die, Jesus emerges from Pilate's praetorium to embark upon the grim procession to Golgotha. The way to the place of execution becomes a path of suffering and compassion, as Jesus endures scourging, mocking, and the weight of the cross. Along the Via Dolorosa, Simon of Cyrene is compelled to bear the beam, and the tears of Jerusalem's mourning women flow freely. Each step manifests the intersection of cruelty and grace—soldiers hiss and jeer, yet Jesus pauses to comfort the afflicted. The path itself, marked by stations of suffering, symbolizes the burden of sin that Christ carries on behalf of humanity. By walking this road, He enacts every prophecy and typology of sacrificial atonement. The way of the cross thus becomes not only a historical route but a spiritual itinerary for all who follow Him.

2.4.1 The Scourging and Mocking of the King

Before the march to Calvary, Jesus endures a brutal scourging: Roman soldiers lash Him repeatedly, tearing flesh and exposing bone (John 19:1; Isaiah 53:5). After His bloodied body is stripped, they clothe Him in purple, place a crown of thorns on His head, and salute Him mockingly as "King of the Jews" (Mark 15:16–20). This grotesque coronation perverts royal imagery, transforming it into the ultimate humiliation. Yet, in this mockery, the truth shines forth: Jesus is indeed King, enthroned on a cross rather than a throne. The contrast between the soldiers' cruelty and the prophet's words—"they have pierced my hands and my feet" (Psalm 22:16)— reinforces the Messianic dimensions of suffering. In this ritual of mock-royalty, divine sovereignty is proclaimed amid scorn.

2.4.2 Bearing the Cross

Commanded to carry His own crossbeam, Jesus staggers under its weight, emblematic of bearing the sins of the world (John 19:17; 1 Peter 2:24). His labored steps reflect not weakness but willing sacrifice, as He moves toward the place of purpose. Each stumble and rise along the rocky path highlights the physical toll of divine love. Passersby, in varying degrees of response, either gawk in curiosity, mock in cruelty, or weep in sympathy. The cross, once a symbol of shame, becomes the instrument of salvation. As Jesus carries the beam, He embodies the prophecy: "He was wounded for our transgressions" (Isaiah 53:5). Believers retrace these footsteps in spiritual solidarity, acknowledging the cost of redemption.

2.4.3 Simon of Cyrene Drafted to Help

At a point along the journey, Roman soldiers compel Simon of Cyrene, a passerby, to shoulder the cross for Jesus (Mark 15:21; Luke 23:26). This act underscores the magnitude of Christ's suffering—He alone could not bear the full weight. Tradition holds that Simon's sons later became prominent figures in the Jerusalem church, suggesting that his brief encounter with Jesus bore lasting fruit. Simon's intervention foreshadows the invitation extended to all: "Take up your cross and follow me" (Matthew 16:24). In bearing the cross, the believer participates in Christ's self-giving, finding identity and purpose in shared sacrifice. Simon's role, though minor in the narrative, becomes a powerful symbol of discipleship.

2.4.4 The Weeping Women of Jerusalem

Amid the jeers, a group of women mourn for Jesus, their tears mingling with the dust of the road (Luke 23:27–31). Jesus pauses and addresses them, saying, "Daughters of Jerusalem, do not weep for me, but weep for yourselves and for your children" (Luke 23:28). His words shift the focus from personal pity to a prophetic lament over coming judgment. The women's sorrow testifies to compassion amid cruelty, while Jesus' response reveals His concern for future generations.

This encounter highlights that grief in the face of injustice can become a catalyst for repentance and transformation. The women's weeping thus remains a poignant witness to the cost and compassion inherent in the way of the cross.

2.5 The Crucifixion Event

Upon reaching Golgotha—"the place of the skull"—Jesus is crucified between two criminals, fulfilling the imagery of Isaiah's suffering Servant (Mark 15:22–27; Isaiah 53). Nails pierce His hands and feet, fastening Him to the wood, while a placard declares Him "King of the Jews" (John 19:19–22). Throughout six hours of agonizing exposure, Jesus utters seven statements—words of forgiveness, promise, and fulfillment—that guide the faithful into deeper appreciation of His mission. As darkness falls over the land and the temple veil tears in two, cosmic realities shift in response to His death. A Roman centurion, observing these signs, confesses, "Truly this man was the Son of God" (Mark 15:39). In these moments of physical horror and spiritual revelation, the cross stands at the intersection of heaven and earth, of judgment and grace.

2.5.1 Nailing and Raising of the Cross

The process of crucifixion begins with the binding of Jesus to the crossbeam, followed by the hammering of nails through wrists and feet (Luke 23:33; John 20:25). The soldiers hoist the beam onto upright posts, letting the weight of His body wrench at the wounds. Each breath becomes a laborious gasp, each exhalation accompanied by anguish. The crowning humiliation and physical torment coalesce into the final act of sacrificial love. Witnesses stand at a distance, some curious, others horrified, as the Son of God is lifted up. In this moment, the weight of human sin hangs visibly upon Christ, yet He endures, fulfilling the promise to bear iniquity (Isaiah 53:6). The raising of the cross transforms wood and torture into the means of eternal redemption.

2.5.2 The Seven Last Words

During His time on the cross, Jesus speaks seven phrases that encapsulate His mission and ministry. First, He prays for forgiveness for His executioners: "Father, forgive them, for they know not what they do" (Luke 23:34). Then He offers salvation to the penitent thief: "Truly, I say to you, today you will be with me in Paradise" (Luke 23:43). To His mother and John, He entrusts a new family of faith: "Woman, behold your son...Behold your mother" (John 19:26–27). Overcome by forsakenness, He cries, "My God, my God, why have you forsaken me?" (Matthew 27:46). Thirsting, He declares, "I thirst" (John 19:28). With triumphant completion, He proclaims, "It is finished" (John 19:30). Finally, surrendering His spirit, He prays, "Father, into your hands I commit my spirit" (Luke 23:46). These utterances reveal forgiveness, promise, love, anguish, fulfillment, and surrender—the full spectrum of redemptive purpose.

2.5.3 Darkness Over the Land

From the sixth hour to the ninth hour, a darkness covers the land, prompting fear and speculation among onlookers (Matthew 27:45; Mark 15:33). This cosmic sign symbolizes divine judgment and the weight of sin borne by the Savior. In Jewish tradition, darkness often signals God's presence or wrath (Amos 8:9). As creation itself responds to the moment of atonement, the universe acknowledges the gravity of Christ's sacrifice. The darkness also heightens the drama of the crucifixion, intensifying the sense that something unprecedented is unfolding. In this shroud, the world enters the mystery of divine exchange—sin for righteousness, death for life.

2.5.4 The Tearing of the Temple Veil

At the moment of Jesus' death, the curtain of the temple— separating the Holy Place from the Most Holy Place—tears in two from top to bottom (Matthew 27:51; Mark 15:38). This dramatic event signals the end of the Old Covenant separation between God and humanity. No longer is access to God mediated solely by priests; through Christ's sacrifice, all believers may draw near with confidence (Hebrews 10:19–22). The tearing from "top to bottom" underscores divine agency rather than human effort. In one gesture, centuries of ritual distancing yield to immediate fellowship. The open way into God's presence stands as a testament to the new relationship secured by the blood of the Lamb.

2.5.5 The Centurion's Confession

Amid these signs, a Roman centurion charged with overseeing the execution proclaims, "Truly this man was the Son of God" (Mark 15:39; Luke 23:47). Coming from a Gentile soldier steeped in the culture of imperial power, this confession carries profound weight. It acknowledges Christ's identity not only in Jewish terms but on a universal stage. The centurion's words serve as an unexpected affirmation that contrasts with the scorn of religious leaders and the derision of the crowd. His testimony reveals that recognition of divine truth often arises in the most unlikely quarters. By confessing Jesus' sonship at the cross, the centurion models the faith to which believers are called—to see beyond external scandal to the glory of the crucified King.

2.6 The Death and Immediate Aftermath

With Jesus' final breath—"It is finished" (John 19:30)—the work of redemption is complete, yet the story does not end in silent stillness. The earth trembles, rocks split, and tombs break open as God's power reverberates through creation (Matthew 27:51–53). Some resuscitated saints appear in Jerusalem, witnessing firsthand the dawn of resurrection life. The centurion and those with him fall on their faces, overwhelmed by awe and fear. Women who had followed Jesus from Galilee stand at a distance, witnessing the tragedy from afar. Amid the chaos, Joseph of Arimathea steps forward to request Jesus' body, setting in motion the burial events that will lead to the empty tomb. These immediate aftermaths foreshadow the seismic shift that Easter morning will bring, when death's power is fully undone.

2.6.1 Jesus' Final Breath

After six hours of agony, Jesus bows His head and yields His spirit to the Father (Luke 23:46). This act of voluntary surrender underscores His authority over life and death. Unlike ordinary crucifixion victims who linger unconscious, Jesus "hands over the spirit," indicating purposeful control (John 19:30). His final words fulfill Scripture and echo the Psalmist's trust in God's sustaining presence (Psalm 31:5). In releasing His spirit, Jesus completes the atonement, bridging heaven and earth once for all (Hebrews 9:12). This breath becomes the hinge of history, shifting humanity's destiny from despair to hope.

2.6.2 The Earthquake and Resurrected Saints

At the moment of death, the ground shakes violently, splitting rocks and opening tombs (Matthew 27:51–52). Many bodies of the saints who had fallen asleep are raised, and after Jesus' resurrection they enter the holy city, appearing to many. This surprising development foreshadows the general resurrection at the end of the age (Daniel 12:2). It testifies that Jesus' death unleashes a power that transcends individual salvation, touching even those who had died centuries earlier. The resurrected saints serve as a foretaste of the new creation, illustrating that death is a temporary condition, undone by divine command. Their appearance in Jerusalem would have provided tangible evidence to early believers of the reality of life beyond the grave.

2.6.3 The Decision of the Crowd

In the aftermath, witnesses respond in varied ways: the centurion confesses faith, while others remain silent or return to ignorance (Matthew 27:54–56). Some women—Mary Magdalene, Mary the mother of James, and Salome—observe from a distance, their steadfast loyalty contrasting with the disciples' earlier flight (Mark 15:40–41). These faithful few bear witness to the burial and later to the empty tomb (Luke 24:10). The divergent responses highlight the human capacity to see or to refuse the signs of God's work. In their decision—

belief or unbelief—each person becomes part of the unfolding drama of redemption. The seeds of the resurrection message take root amid these mourning witnesses, who will carry the story forward.

2.7 Burial and the Guarded Tomb

As the sun sinks on Good Friday, Joseph of Arimathea—a respected member of the council—boldly petitions Pilate for Jesus' body (Mark 15:42–46). Assisted by Nicodemus, he wraps the body in linen with myrrh and aloes, preparing it for burial (John 19:39–40). They lay Jesus in a new tomb hewn from rock, rolling a great stone to seal the entrance (Matthew 27:57–60). To prevent theft or further unrest, the chief priests secure a guard and set a seal on the stone (Matthew 27:62–66). Thus, the tomb becomes both a prison and a fortress: guarded, sealed, and watched. Yet, as this chapter will show, no guard can ultimately hold the risen Lord. The burial rituals—spices, wrapping, stone—prepare the way for the wondrous discovery of the empty tomb on the third day.

2.7.1 Joseph of Arimathea's Request

In a remarkable act of courage, Joseph approaches Pilate immediately after Jesus' death, requesting His corpse (Mark 15:43). As a member of the Sanhedrin who had not consented to Jesus' condemnation, Joseph distinguishes himself by providing a burial fit for a king. This gesture fulfills Isaiah's prophecy: "He was assigned a grave with the wicked, and with the rich in his death" (Isaiah 53:9). Joseph's actions reflect repentance and reverence, as he publicly identifies with Jesus in death. His willingness to risk association with a condemned man underscores the transformative power of Christ's ministry. In offering his own tomb, Joseph becomes a vessel of God's compassion in the face of shame.

2.7.2 Nicodemus Brings Spices

Nicodemus, who had earlier come to Jesus by night, now brings a mixture of myrrh and aloes—about seventy-five pounds—to anoint the body (John 19:39–40). These costly spices illustrate the honor bestowed upon the deceased and the depth of devotion held by Jesus' followers. Their presence echoes the prophetic tradition of burial anointing (Psalm 45:7; Isaiah 61:1). Yet, the spices also highlight the finality of death: elaborate preparation cannot prevent corruption. In their act of love, Joseph and Nicodemus model that devotion to Christ extends beyond words to sacrificial service. Their collaboration foreshadows the global fellowship that will gather around the risen Lord.

2.7.3 The Rolling of the Stone

After laying the body in the rock-hewn tomb, Joseph rolls a great stone across the entrance (Matthew 27:59–60). This sealing signifies both closure and security: closure of Jesus' earthly ministry and security against tampering. The physical barrier underscores the reality of death's finality. Yet for believers, the sealed stone anticipates the miracle soon to unfold: the stone will be rolled away by divine power, not human might (Matthew 28:2–4). In the interim, the seal becomes a testimony to the authorities' fear of Jesus' influence, even in death. The stone thus marks the boundary between death's dominion and life's impending triumph.

2.7.4 The Roman Guard and the Seal

At the request of Jewish leaders, Pilate stations a guard at the tomb and provides a seal to prevent the disciples from stealing the body (Matthew 27:62–66). The combination of armed soldiers and imperial seal underscores the perceived threat of Jesus' proclamation, even in death. Ironically, these measures only serve to confirm the truth of the resurrection when the guards report the empty tomb (Matthew 28:11–15). The seal, intended to imprison, becomes a symbol of divine escape; the guard, intended to deter, becomes a witness to the power that overcame death. In this way, human efforts to contain Jesus backfire, highlighting that the risen Lord transcends every barrier.

Conclusion The way of the cross charts a course through betrayal, unjust condemnation, excruciating suffering, and solemn burial—and yet each milestone bears the imprint of divine sovereignty and redemptive intent. From the covenantal promise in the Upper Room to the weighty silence of the sealed tomb, every act, word, and sign points beyond itself to the greater miracle awaiting Easter dawn. Through His voluntary submission, Jesus satisfies the demands of justice; through His sacrificial death, He secures the blessings of mercy; and through His burial, He models the certainty of resurrection life. The layers of prophecy fulfilled, the echoes of creation shuddering, the tears of faithful women, and the astonishment of hardened soldiers all testify that God is at work even in what appears most final. As we reflect on this journey—rich in theology and grim in reality—our hopes are anchored in the truth that the cross is not the end but the gateway to new creation. May this deepened appreciation of the Passion prepare our hearts to rejoice with the dawn of resurrection.

Chapter 3: The Empty Tomb—Gospel Narratives Compared

The discovery of the empty tomb stands at the very heart of Christian proclamation. In the early hours of the first day of the week, a group of faithful women arrived at the burial site of Jesus, expecting sorrow but finding astonishment. Their encounter with an open grave was not merely a curious historical accident but the dawn of a new reality in which death no longer held ultimate sway. Each Gospel writer preserves this pivotal event with distinctive details and emphases, yet all converge on the central truth that Jesus rose bodily from the dead. In the chapters to follow, we will compare and contrast Mark's austere brevity, Luke's theological depth, Matthew's dramatic flourishes, and John's intimate portrait, discerning how each narrative invites readers into the wonder of resurrection. By examining the testimonies in parallel, we gain a richer, multi-faceted understanding of how God validated Christ's identity, vindicated His mission, and inaugurated the age to come. As we trace these Gospel accounts side by side, may our own faith be deepened and our witness galvanized by the reality of the risen Lord.

3.1 The Women's Discovery at Dawn

Each Gospel begins its empty-tomb narrative with a dawn visit by women who had followed Jesus from Galilee. Their predawn journey underscores both urgency and vulnerability: they carried spices to anoint a body already sealed by Roman decree. The timing "very early, while it was still dark" (John 20:1) situates the discovery in liminal space, where night yields to light—a fitting metaphor for resurrection itself. All four Gospels highlight the women's role as the first witnesses, overturning contemporary expectations that minimized female testimony. Their faithfulness in death's domain contrasts with the disciples' flight at Gethsemane, foreshadowing how God often entrusts truth to the humble and marginalized. As the women approached, Scripture emphasizes God's initiative: stones rolled away, angels appeared, and utterance of divine proclamation. In this section, we survey the four portraits of these devoted followers, noting how each Evangelist shapes their encounter to convey theological insight and narrative momentum.

3.1.1 Mark's Brief but Powerful Note

Mark's account of the empty tomb (Mark 16:1–8) is striking in its brevity and immediacy. He mentions only three women— Mary Magdalene, Mary the mother of James, and Salome— underscoring a tight circle of faithful witnesses. Mark emphasizes the abruptness of God's action: "They went to the tomb at dawn… and saw that the stone… had been rolled away" (Mark 16:2–4). Rather than focusing on dialogue, Mark foregrounds the women's visceral reaction: fear and astonishment (Mark 16:5–8). The lone young man in white commands them to proclaim the message of resurrection to the disciples, then they flee in silence, overcome by terror. Mark's abrupt ending—"for they were afraid" (v. 8)—leaves the reader suspended in the tension between divine triumph and human dread. In this compressed narrative, Mark powerfully conveys that the resurrection shatters expectations in such a way that even the first responders cannot immediately process its significance.

3.1.2 Luke's Detailed Account and Theological Emphasis

Luke's narration (Luke 24:1–11) expands both cast and context, naming Joanna alongside Mary Magdalene and Mary the mother of James. He underscores their logistical concern: "Who will roll away the stone for us?" (Luke 24:2), only to highlight God's preemptive care in removing it. Luke introduces two "men in dazzling apparel" who echo Christ's own words: "Why do you seek the living among the dead?" (Luke 24:5–6). This theological question reframes the women's expectations, reminding them that resurrection transcends all categories of murder and burial. Luke also emphasizes the reliability of testimony: the women "returned from the tomb and told all these things to the eleven and to all the rest" (v. 9), though "their words seemed to them an idle tale" (v. 11). By presenting the disciples' initial skepticism, Luke models the process by which faith emerges from hearing and pondering Scripture. His account weaves together historical detail and theological reflection, portraying the empty tomb not only as an event but as a fulfillment of prophetic narrative.

3.1.3 Matthew's Dramatic Unfolding

Matthew's version (Matthew 28:1–10) begins with an earthquake and the descent of an angel "like lightning" (v. 3), enveloped in "white as snow" garments (v. 3). This cosmic disturbance underscores the magnitude of resurrection, as creation itself responds. The angel rolls back the stone with authoritative ease and invites the women—again Mary Magdalene and the other Mary—to "come, see the place where he lay" (v. 6). Before they can fully comprehend, Jesus Himself appears, greeting them: "Greetings!" (v. 9), and they clasp His feet in worship. Matthew then pairs divine and human messengers: the angel commissions them to "go and tell my brothers" (v. 10), situating the resurrection as both cosmic wonder and relational summons. By juxtaposing terror with joy—"they departed quickly with fear and great joy" (v. 8)—Matthew crafts a dynamic tableau that underscores how resurrection ignites both awe and obedient witness in the community.

3.1.4 John's Intimate Portrait of Mary Magdalene

John's Gospel (John 20:1–2) zeroes in on Mary Magdalene, presenting her as the first to arrive, alone and "weeping" (v. 11). Her emotional distress highlights the personal loss she had suffered and the depth of her devotion. She discovers the stone removed and the tomb empty, then hastens to inform Peter and the beloved disciple: "They have taken the Lord out of the tomb, and we do not know where they have laid him" (v. 2). John's focus on interpersonal relationships—Mary's dialogue with Peter and "the other disciple"—prepares for a shifting of roles from mourner to messenger. His narrative style underscores that resurrection begins in the heart, as Mary moves from despair to missionary impulse. By concentrating on a single figure, John invites readers to experience the discovery as a personal encounter. The intimate portrait of grief transformed into proclamation illustrates how resurrection reshapes individual lives as well as communal memory.

3.2 Angelic Encounters and Divine Messengers

Each Gospel characterizes divine intervention at the tomb through angelic agents, yet their number, appearance, and message vary, reflecting each author's theological emphasis. Angels serve as God's emissaries, bridging heavenly reality and human experience, announcing that death has been defeated. In Mark, a solitary young man symbolizes the singular authority of Christ's resurrection. Luke presents two figures, evoking completeness and echoing Sinai's theophany. Matthew combines a dramatic celestial descent with the terror of a Roman guard, while John situates angels within a garden-tomb milieu, preparing the stage for personal revelation. By comparing these portrayals, we discern how angelic presence both confirms divine sovereignty over the grave and commissions human witnesses to bear the good news. The angels' words shift the narrative from despair to proclamation, reminding readers that resurrection is God's initiative, announced through created beings to effect redemptive purposes among fallen humanity.

3.2.1 The Single Young Man in Mark

Mark's terse description (Mark 16:5–7) depicts a lone young man "in a white robe" seated on the right side of the tomb entrance. His positioning on the right hand signifies honor and authority, echoing Old Testament imagery of enthronement (Psalm 110:1). The young man's calm command—"Do not be alarmed; you seek Jesus of Nazareth, who was crucified. He has risen; he is not here" (Mark 16:6)—melds comfort with proclamation, dispelling terror with divine assurance. His directive to "go, tell his disciples and Peter" underscores both the communal and personal dimensions of witness, as Peter's earlier denial is offset by this special mention. Mark's angelic figure, though singular, encapsulates the power of resurrection and the necessity of human obedience. By omitting elaborate description, Mark invites readers to focus on the message rather than the messenger, emphasizing that the core marvel lies in the risen Christ, not in celestial ceremony.

3.2.2 Two Men in White in Luke

Luke's double-angel motif (Luke 24:4–7) resonates with symbolic fullness: two witnesses provide corroboration (Deuteronomy 19:15), and the pair evokes the cherubim that guard the divine presence (Exodus 25:18–22). Luke's men "in dazzling apparel" interrupt the women's lament with the probing question: "Why do you seek the living among the dead?" (Luke 24:5). Their response weaves together past prophecy and present fulfillment: "He is not here, but has risen. Remember how he told you…" (v. 6–7). By citing Jesus' own predictions, the angels root resurrection within Christ's self-revelation, framing the event as the climax of God's redemptive script. Luke's pluralization underscores communal testimony, aligning heavenly witnesses with earthbound disciples. Their rapid disappearance after speaking mirrors the invisible yet palpable presence of God at work. In this account, the angels serve as theologians, emphasizing that resurrection is both theologically coherent and experientially transformative.

3.2.3 Matthew's Earthquake-Angel, Guard Terror, and Commission

Matthew intensifies the scene (Matthew 28:2–7) by coupling cosmic disturbance—a great earthquake—with an angel descending "from heaven" whose appearance was "like lightning" (v. 3). This powerful imagery underscores that resurrection is a universe-shaking event, transcending human and natural orders. The angel's face "like lightning" and his clothing "white as snow" evoke purity and divine radiance, reminiscent of the Transfiguration (Matthew 17:2). In fear, the guards "became like dead men" (v. 4), illustrating that the power of God's messenger surpasses martial might. By rolling back the stone himself, the angel both demonstrates authority over death's barrier and invites human witnesses to enter. His proclamation—"He is not here; for he has risen" (v. 6)—combines affirmation of absence with rubric of presence. Finally, the angel commissions the women to "go quickly and tell his disciples" (v. 7), linking divine announcement to apostolic mission and establishing the resurrection as the foundation of church witness.

3.2.4 John's Unrecognized Messenger and Mary's Turn

In John's narrative (John 20:11–13), Mary Magdalene remains outside the tomb, weeping, until she stoops to peer inside and sees two angels "in white, sitting where the body of Jesus had lain." Their silent question—"Woman, why are you weeping?"—mirrors Jesus' later address, forging a literary and theological connection between angelic and Christic presence. The angels occupy positions "one at the head and one at the feet," reminiscent of the cherubic symbolism that signifies divine throne room (Exodus 25:20). John's emphasis on Mary's grief and the angels' compassionate inquiry creates an intimate setting, preparing her heart for the greater revelation. Their brief role highlights that resurrection unfolds through both heavenly dialogue and personal encounter. By omitting elaborate angelic speech, John focuses attention on Mary's call to look deeper, teaching readers that resurrection is apprehended not through spectacle alone but through relational invitation.

3.3 Peter and John at the Tomb

Following the women's report, Peter and the beloved disciple race to the tomb, each displaying distinctive responses that complement the women's initial discovery. Peter's impulsive entry and John's contemplative inspection underscore two modes of encountering resurrection: active investigation and reflective faith. Their observations of the linen wrappings and face cloth serve as crucial evidences, pointing away from body theft and toward divine agency. By noting how the grave clothes lay neatly folded, the disciples discern that the missing body reflects purposeful zeal rather than hurried escape. This joint yet differentiated testimony bridges the first annunciation by the women and subsequent personal revelations by Jesus Himself. In this section, we explore how Peter's courage, John's belief, and the significance of grave clothes converge to broaden the narrative of resurrection from communal proclamation to doctrinal foundation.

3.3.1 Peter's Bold Entry and Immediate Wonder

Luke notes that Peter "got up and ran to the tomb; stooping and looking in, he saw the linen cloths by themselves; and he went home marveling at what had happened" (Luke 24:12). Peter's haste underscores his leadership role and his zeal to see the truth for himself. His entry into the tomb, unaccompanied by caution or fear, contrasts sharply with the women's initial trepidation. Observing the cloths "by themselves" suggests that the body's absence was not a result of grave robbery; criminals would not have neatly unwound burial wrappings. Peter's marveling rather than explicit faith indicates an intermediate stage—he is intrigued but not yet fully comprehending the theological implications. His wonder models a posture of openness, inviting readers to approach resurrection with curiosity and expectant humility. Furthermore, Peter's solitary reflection paves the way for later personal encounters with the risen Christ, framing resurrection as an invitation to deeper discipleship.

3.3.2 John's Believing Witness

John, arriving second but entering first, "saw and believed" (John 20:8), connecting visual evidence to personal conviction. His belief emerges from contemplative scrutiny: he notes not only the linen cloths "lying there" but also the face cloth "rolled up in a place by itself" (v. 7). The orderly arrangement of burial cloths, including the separate face wrap, speaks to intentional divine action rather than chaotic removal. John's belief "before they understood the Scripture" (v. 9) underscores that faith often precedes full doctrinal comprehension. By characterizing John as the "disciple whom Jesus loved," the Gospel underscores the role of relational intimacy in catalyzing faith. His quiet confidence contrasts with Peter's outward wonder, illustrating complementary facets of resurrection response—both active amazement and reflective trust. John's testimony becomes a paradigmatic witness, bridging the gap between historical fact and personal faith in the risen Lord.

3.3.3 Significance of the Linen Wrappings

The Gospel narratives converge on the detail of grave clothes, a feature with deep theological resonance. In first-century Judea, burial involved wrapping the body in linen cloths, often accompanied by spices (John 19:40; Luke 23:53). The presence of these wrappings, undisturbed and neatly arranged, argues against hasty removal or theft. Rather, they point toward a resurrection event that preserves bodily continuity while transcending death's finality. Early church tradition—from Justin Martyr to the accounts of the Shroud—grappled with the significance of these cloths, viewing them as silent sermons on divine order and intentional rebirth. The unwrapped body suggests that Jesus passed through the grave clothes rather than being removed, indicating a transformed, imperishable life (1 Corinthians 15:42–44). This motif invites reflection on how God transforms the remnants of death into testimonies of new creation. Thus, linen wrappings function as theological signposts within the tomb, guiding believers toward a robust understanding of bodily resurrection.

3.4 Mary Magdalene's Personal Encounter

Beyond group experiences and angelic announcements, John emphasizes a singular, intimate encounter between Mary Magdalene and the risen Jesus. Her transformation from grief to mission encapsulates the personal power of resurrection revelation. By addressing her by name, Jesus underscores relational recognition and restoration. This one-on-one moment becomes the prototypical encounter for all who seek Christ in sorrow. Mary's subsequent commissioning as "apostle to the apostles" demonstrates that resurrection commissions transcend gender and social status, ushering in a new egalitarian community. In this section, we examine how Mary's journey from mourning to mission unfolds, and how her experience contrasts with other Gospel witnesses, highlighting the multi-dimensional nature of resurrection encounters.

3.4.1 From Mourning to Mission

John relates that Mary remained at the tomb weeping until two angels asked, "Woman, why are you weeping?" (John 20:13). Her focus on the missing body underscores her unyielding loyalty and grief. Turning, she sees Jesus standing but does not recognize him immediately, mistaking him for the gardener (v. 14–15). Only when he calls her name—"Mary"—does recognition break forth, prompting her exclamation, "Rabboni!" (v. 16). This moment of naming signifies deeply personal restoration; Jesus calls her by the intimate form of address, recalling shared moments of ministry. He then commissions her: "Do not cling to me…go to my brothers and say to them, 'I am ascending to my Father'" (v. 17). Empowered by this charge, Mary departs to declare: "I have seen the Lord" (v. 18). Thus, her encounter shifts from private encounter to public proclamation, modeling how resurrection transforms mourning disciples into heralds of hope.

3.4.2 Contrasts with Other Gospel Witnesses

While the Synoptic Gospels emphasize group discovery, John's focus on Mary Magdalene highlights the individual dimension of resurrection encounter. The two angels in John prompt Mary's attention inward, preparing her heart for Christ's revelation. Unlike Matthew's duet of Marys or Luke's larger band, John isolates Mary to emphasize relational intimacy. Where Matthew includes worship and physical touch—clasping Jesus' feet—John narrates a spiritual commissioning without physical contact. Mary's unique role as lone witness to Christ's first appearance sets her apart, prefiguring the inclusive scope of the church's mission. Her immediate obedience contrasts with the disciples' initial unbelief, illustrating that resurrection revelations often bypass established leaders. In Mary's transformation, we observe how resurrection encounters can be intensely personal, yet carry universal implications for mission and community.

3.5 The Guarded Tomb: Human Pretensions and Divine Triumph

Matthew uniquely reports that the Jewish authorities, fearing disciples might steal the body, secured the tomb by sealing the stone and posting a guard (Matthew 27:62–66). This human attempt to contain Jesus' influence only magnifies the power of resurrection when guards witness—or fall victim to—divine intervention. The seal, intended to enforce permanence, becomes a day-break barrier broken by angelic might. Attempts at cover-up further expose human fear in contrast to God's unstoppable purposes. The narrative of guard report and bribery (Matthew 28:11–15) underscores that resurrection truth cannot be suppressed by political or religious expedience. In this section, we explore how human precautions both acknowledge resurrection's potency and inadvertently confirm its reality, revealing God's sovereignty triumphing over every human strategy.

3.5.1 Securing the Stone and Stationing the Guard

Pilate's authorization to seal the tomb and station a guard represents a dramatic intersection of Roman authority and Jewish concern. The seal, typically a sign of imperial decree, carried lethal penalties if broken, indicating the seriousness with which authorities treated the claim of empty tomb. The presence of a guard of Roman soldiers, highly trained and disciplined, signifies that the world's most formidable force could not forestall the power of God. By requesting these measures, Jewish leaders tacitly affirmed the disciples' potential for stirring popular movements. Yet, these very precautions amplify the wonder when the tomb is found empty despite every human safeguard. The sealed guard duty underscores the conviction that Jesus continued to move crowds even in death. Thus, the story of the guarded tomb becomes a testament to divine triumph over earthly power.

3.5.2 Guard Report and Attempted Cover-Up

When the guards reported the empty tomb to the chief priests, they were bribed to circulate the story that the disciples stole the body while the guards slept (Matthew 28:11–15). This cover-up plot exposes the paradox of human attempts to suppress divine revelation: the more vigorously men strive to bury truth, the more they authenticate its potency by seeking to silence it. The bribe—"if this comes to the governor's ears…"—signals a conspiracy of fear, revealing the authorities' anxiety about Jesus' postmortem influence. Despite the fabricated narrative, the empty tomb remained an affront to all human control, as the real story spread through testimony rather than force. Matthew's inclusion of this episode serves to strengthen the historical credibility of the empty-tomb tradition, demonstrating how early opponents felt compelled to deny what they could not refute. Ultimately, the cover-up backfires, as attempts at deception underscore the irresistible reality of resurrection.

3.6 Harmonizing the Four Gospel Accounts

Reconciling the four Gospel narratives of the empty tomb invites careful attention to chronology, detail, and theological emphasis. Apparent discrepancies—such as the number of angels, the sequence of events, or the presence of guards—yield to a harmonized reading that respects each author's intent. By mapping dawn visits, angelic actions, and disciple responses, a composite timeline emerges that accommodates variation without contradiction. Number symbolism and narrative focus reveal how Mark accentuates mystery, Luke emphasizes scriptural fulfillment, Matthew underscores authority, and John highlights personal encounter. Integrating these perspectives yields a panoramic view of resurrection that is both historically grounded and theologically rich. In this section, we explore methods of harmonization, demonstrating how diverse testimonies converge to affirm the empty tomb as an event of first importance.

3.6.1 Chronological Harmonies

A harmonized chronology suggests that the stone may have been rolled back before the women's arrival or in their presence, and that angelic proclamations and Christ's own appearance overlapped in rapid sequence. For instance, Mark's abrupt note of the stone's removal aligns with Matthew's angelic descent causing an earthquake, while Luke's "two men in dazzling apparel" correspond to John's description of angels seated within. The women's hurry to tell the disciples follows immediately, prompting Peter and John's investigation. Weaving these sequences together—early dawn, stone removal, angelic announcement, Christ's appearance, disciple inspection—yields a coherent narrative flow. Recognizing that each evangelist tailors time markers to theological purpose allows readers to appreciate consistency in core facts despite literary variation. Chronological harmonization thus enriches rather than diminishes confidence in the Gospel record.

3.6.2 Reconciling Angelic Numbers and Descriptions

The variation in angelic witnesses—one young man in Mark, two men in Luke, one angel plus guard in Matthew, two angels in John—reflects distinct theological motifs rather than factual discord. Mark's solitary figure points to Christ's singular authority; Luke's pair echoes covenantal witness and echoes Sinai's revelation; Matthew's angelic and human elements highlight cosmic and civic reaction; John's cherubic seating evokes divine presence in a garden setting. By recognizing the symbolic language at work—such as the significance of two as completeness or of numbers echoing Old Testament patterns—harmonists discern that discrepancies serve thematic ends. The differences invite reflection on how God reveals the same truth through varied literary lenses, enriching the tapestry of testimony. In this way, angelic multiplicity becomes a complementary chorus rather than a competitive roster.

3.6.3 Integrating Unique Theological Emphases

Each Gospel writer shapes the empty-tomb narrative to highlight aspects of Christ's person and mission. Mark underscores mystery and urgency, leaving readers in contemplative tension. Luke emphasizes fulfillment of Scripture and careful witness, framing resurrection within God's redemptive drama. Matthew magnifies authority—cosmic, angelic, and apostolic—sealing the narrative with worship. John personalizes the resurrection, focusing on relational recognition and commissioning. Integrating these emphases yields a multi-dimensional portrayal: the resurrection is mysterious yet scripturally grounded, authoritative yet personal. Harmonization honors authorial diversity, allowing each perspective to contribute distinct hues to the portrait of the risen Lord. Through this synthesis, the empty tomb emerges as a multifaceted jewel, refracting divine glory into every corner of the Christian narrative.

3.7 The Empty Tomb in Early Christian Proclamation

The early church's preaching and teaching rapidly centered the empty tomb as foundational to faith. At Pentecost, Peter declared, "God has made him both Lord and Christ, this Jesus whom you crucified" (Acts 2:36), citing Psalm 16's promise that the Holy One would not see decay (Acts 2:25–32). In Corinth, Paul affirmed the resurrection's primacy: "If Christ has not been raised, your faith is futile" (1 Corinthians 15:17–19), grounding his argument in the historical reality of an empty grave. Creedal statements—from the Didache to the Apostles' Creed—presuppose Jesus' rising, integrating it into baptismal confession and liturgical practice. Hymns and Easter rites continually recall the stone rolled away, while art and architecture frame worship space around the tomb motif. The empty tomb thus transcended biography, becoming a sacramental symbol in liturgy, a polemic in apologetics, and a catalyst for missionary boldness. In this section, we trace how the earliest believers leveraged the empty tomb in preaching, doctrine, and worship, making it the hinge of Christian identity.

3.7.1 Peter's Pentecost Sermon

On the day of Pentecost, Peter appeals to Old Testament prophecy in Psalm 16 to interpret Jesus' resurrection, declaring that David spoke of Christ's rising (Acts 2:29–32). His sermon links the empty tomb with divine vindication, affirming that death could not hold God's Anointed. Peter's bold proclamation spurs three thousand to repentance and baptism, illustrating how resurrection preaching ignites communal transformation (Acts 2:41). By framing resurrection as fulfillment of Scripture, Peter roots the new covenant in God's unbreakable promises. His use of the empty tomb underscores that faith is anchored in historical events, not merely private experience. The sermon models apostolic strategy: scriptural exposition leading to Christ-centered proclamation, culminating in ecclesial formation.

3.7.2 Paul's Affirmation in Corinth

In 1 Corinthians 15:3–8, Paul lists eyewitnesses to the risen Christ—Cephas, the twelve, over five hundred brethren, James, and finally Paul himself—underscoring the resurrection's historic and communal dimensions. His credo places the resurrection alongside Christ's death and burial as "of first importance" (v. 3–4). Paul's argument hinges on the empty-tomb fact; without it, he asserts, preaching and faith are "futile" (v. 14,17). By demonstrating how burial and rising form a chiastic structure—Christ died for sins, was buried, and rose on the third day—Paul integrates narrative and theology. His teaching clarifies that bodily resurrection will extend to believers (v. 20–23), linking Christ's victory with the hope of new life. In Corinth, a city rife with philosophical skepticism, the empty tomb serves as unstoppable proof against those who claimed resurrection a mere spiritual metaphor.

3.7.3 Creedal and Liturgical Reflections

Early Christian creeds crystallize the empty tomb into concise confessions: "He died under Pontius Pilate, was buried, and on the third day rose again according to the Scriptures." The Didache (late 1st century) instructs baptism in "the name of the Father and of the Son and of the Holy Spirit," grounding new life in the resurrection event. Easter liturgies regularly narrate the tomb story, reenacted through hymns like the Exsultet and the Paschal greeting, "Christ is risen! He is risen indeed!" Church art—catacomb frescoes, medieval paintings, modern stained glass—centers the vacant tomb as icon of hope. These practices embed the empty tomb in the rhythm of worship, ensuring that each generation encounters the resurrection not only as doctrine but as experiential reality. Through liturgy and creed, the empty tomb becomes the beating heart of Christian memory and anticipation.

3.8 Archaeological and Historical Context

While the Gospel writers focus on theological witness, archaeological and historical research provides cultural and material context that affirms their descriptions. First-century Jewish burial customs involved rock-cut tombs, ossuaries, and elaborate anointing with spices—details reflected in Gospel accounts of linen wrappings and aromatic preparations. Rolling stones functioned as practical seals to prevent intrusion and tampering. Roman military protocols forbade guards from sleeping on duty, making the guards' collapse under divine presence a moment of narrative power. Early pilgrims to Jerusalem identified tomb sites—such as the Church of the Holy Sepulchre and the Garden Tomb—suggesting an enduring tradition anchored in geography. While precise localization remains debated, the convergence of textual detail and archaeological patterns lends credibility to Gospel depictions. In this section, we examine burial practices, guard protocols, and the garden-tomb tradition to ground the empty-tomb narratives in historical reality.

3.8.1 First-Century Jewish Burial Customs

Contemporary tomb excavations around Jerusalem reveal family tombs hewn into rock, with loculi for bodies and shelves for ossuaries. Deceased individuals were often wrapped in linen with aromatic spices such as myrrh and aloes (John 19:39–40). These practices align with Gospel descriptions, indicating that Jesus' burial followed local custom. The weight and bulk of the spices—reportedly seventy-five pounds—underscore the disciples' devotion and the significance of proper burial. Archaeologists find that gourds or rolling stones served as closures, matching Gospel images of a "great stone." Knowledge of these customs deepens appreciation for how Gospel writers situated the empty tomb within ordinary practices, then imbued them with extraordinary meaning.

3.8.2 Roman Guard Protocols and Seals

Roman military regulations prohibited soldiers from sleeping on duty, punishable by severe penalty, highlighting the dramatic nature of their collapse at the tomb (Matthew 28:4). Imperial seals signified legal authority, often affixed with wax bearing the governor's emblem; breaking such a seal was tantamount to capital offense. Pilate's seal on the tomb thus conveyed both official endorsement of burial and deterrence against tampering. The presence of armed guards and sealed stone underscores the perceived threat of Christ's continued influence even after death. Understanding these protocols affirms the Gospel's historical plausibility and underscores the paradox that God's power overrode every human precaution.

3.8.3 The Garden Tomb Tradition

From the 4th century onward, pilgrims identified sites in Jerusalem as Golgotha and the tomb of Jesus. The Church of the Holy Sepulchre, venerated since Constantine's time, preserves a complex of rocky hill and burial chamber. In the 19th century, the Garden Tomb near Gordon's Calvary emerged as an alternative candidate, noted for its garden-like setting and rolling-stone architecture. While scholarly consensus varies, both sites reflect early Christian veneration of specific locations tied to the empty-tomb narrative. Archaeological surveys and historical geography enrich our understanding of how memory and witness coalesced into tangible places of pilgrimage. These traditions illustrate the empty tomb's enduring spiritual magnetism and its capacity to ground faith in both story and site.

3.9 The Empty Tomb as the Dawn of New Creation

Theologically, the empty tomb signifies not only Christ's personal victory over death but the inauguration of cosmic renewal. Positioned in a garden-tomb, the resurrection narrative evokes Eden's promise and the reversal of the curse pronounced in Genesis 3:17–19. The earthquake at Calvary hints at renewal of the earth itself, as creation groans for liberation (Romans 8:19–22). Early Christians likened the tomb to a womb, from which new life emerges, foreshadowing baptismal imagery of death and rebirth (Romans 6:4). The resurrection of Christ becomes the "firstfruits" (1 Corinthians 15:20) of a harvest that will culminate in new heavens and a new earth (Revelation 21:1–5). By viewing the empty tomb through the lens of creation-renewal, believers perceive a horizon that extends beyond individual salvation to cosmic restoration. In this section, we explore how the empty tomb signals new beginnings, fulfills creation's redemption, and functions as the paradigm for spiritual rebirth.

3.9.1 Symbolism of New Beginnings

The timing of the resurrection "on the first day of the week" (Mark 16:2) evokes the first day of creation when God said, "Let there be light" (Genesis 1:3). Just as light pierced primordial darkness, resurrection ushers in "true light" that overcomes spiritual gloom (John 1:9). The garden setting, with its implicit allusion to Eden, grounds the event in creation imagery. Early Christian hymns spoke of Christ as the "second Adam" whose rising undoes the first Adam's trespass (1 Corinthians 15:45–49). By emerging from a tomb carved out of rock—symbolic of both strength and mortality—Christ inaugurates a new creation order in which death is transmuted into life. This symbolism invites believers to see Easter not merely as historical event but as cosmic watershed, initiating a reign of new beginnings.

3.9.2 Fulfillment of Creation's Redemption

Paul teaches that all creation waits "with eager longing for the revealing of the sons of God" (Romans 8:19), groaning under bondage to corruption. Christ's resurrection is the "firstfruits" of what God will accomplish for creation (1 Corinthians 15:20; Romans 8:22–23). The empty tomb therefore stands as the guarantee (arrabōn) of future bodily resurrection—for individuals and for creation itself (Ephesians 1:14). Christ's rising reverses the downward trajectory set by Adam's fall, aligning creation with its intended destiny. The cosmic dimensions of resurrection fuel Christian stewardship of the earth, as believers live in hope of full restoration. Thus, the empty tomb bridges the gap between personal faith and ecological vision, showing that God's redemptive plan encompasses all he has made.

3.9.3 The Tomb as Womb of Resurrection Life

Early theologians, from Justin Martyr to Gregory of Nyssa, likened the tomb to a womb, portraying resurrection as birth into new life. Liturgical practices—especially baptism—echo this imagery: believers are buried with Christ and raised to walk in newness of life (Romans 6:3–4). Church art frequently depicts Christ emerging from a cracked tomb as a newborn stepping into glory. Monastic writers drew on the womb-tomb parallel to explore the spiritual rebirth that follows repentance. This metaphor emphasizes that resurrection is not simply a reversal of death but a qualitative transformation into imperishable life. By embracing the womb-tomb motif, the church captures the paradox of death-fueled life, inviting every disciple into a continual process of dying and rising with Christ.

Conclusion The Gospel narratives of the empty tomb, when placed side by side, form a kaleidoscope of divine revelation: Mark's austere prompt, Luke's theological richness, Matthew's cosmic drama, and John's intimate encounter. Each account, while distinct in detail, rejoices in the same essential truth—

Jesus Christ rose bodily from the dead, inaugurating redemption for humanity and restoration for creation. The women's faithful discovery, angelic proclamations, the disciples' investigative wonder, and Mary Magdalene's personal commission all converge to affirm resurrection as the hinge of history. Human precautions—sealed stones and armed guards—only underscore God's sovereignty in triumphing over every barrier. Early church proclamation, creedal summaries, liturgical celebrations, and archaeological insights further attest to the empty tomb's enduring potency. In viewing the tomb as the womb of new creation, we embrace a theology that transcends death to birth new hope. As we depart this chapter's mosaic of testimonies, we stand poised to encounter the risen Lord in person, hear His voice, and heed His call to bear the resurrection message into a world longing for life in place of death.

Chapter 4: Encounters with the Risen Lord

The resurrection of Jesus Christ did not conclude with an empty tomb; it inaugurated a series of profound encounters that forever transformed the lives of those who beheld the risen Lord. Each appearance reveals a different dimension of His victory over death—intimate and personal, communal and public, private and prophetic. In these meetings, grief gives way to joy, doubt to faith, despair to mission, and the temporal to the eternal. Through the disciple's touch, the stranger's guidance, and the Master's voice, the early followers discovered that death had lost its sting and life its limitation. Moreover, these post-resurrection moments laid the foundation for the apostolic church's identity, worship, and mission. As we journey through these encounters, we glimpse not only the continuity of Jesus' earthly ministry but also the novelty of His risen presence. May this exploration deepen our own sense of awe and fuel our resolve to live in the light of the One who conquered the grave.

4.1 Individual Appearances

4.1.1 Mary Magdalene in the Garden

Mary Magdalene approached the tomb before sunrise, burdened by sorrow and carrying spices to anoint Jesus' body. As John recounts, she wept outside the tomb until she stooped to look inside and saw two angels in white seats where the Lord's body had been (John 20:11–12). Her tears testified to both her love and her confusion—how could the grave hold the One she cherished? Turning, she caught sight of a man she mistook for the gardener. Only when He spoke her name, "Mary," did recognition ignite within her heart, prompting her to respond, "Rabboni!" (which means Teacher) (John 20:16). In that moment, the barrier between human anguish and divine compassion dissolved, revealing a personal Lord who calls each believer by name. Jesus then entrusted her with the first commission—to go and tell the disciples, "I am ascending to my Father and your Father, to my God and your God" (John 20:17). This intimate appearance underscores that resurrection life begins with relational restoration and personal commissioning.

Mary's encounter also highlights the reversal of roles between sorrow and service. Initially sent to care for Jesus' corpse, she becomes the apostle to the apostles, bearing the good news of resurrection (John 20:18). Her willingness to linger in grief positioned her to receive more than closure; she gained the gift of abiding hope. Furthermore, by choosing a woman as the inaugural witness, the risen Lord subverted societal expectations and affirmed the testimony of the marginalized. Mary's story invites modern readers to recognize that faith often emerges in the crucible of loss and that personal devotion can blossom into powerful witness. As Mary ran to the disciples, joy overtook her sorrow—a pattern repeated in every life transformed by the risen Christ.

4.1.2 Thomas's Touch of Belief

The risen Jesus first appeared to ten of the disciples behind locked doors, but Thomas was absent (John 20:24). When they reported Jesus' visit, Thomas refused to believe unless he could touch the nail wounds and thrust his hand into the pierced side (John 20:25). A week later, Jesus returned and addressed Thomas's doubt directly: "Put your finger here; see my hands. Reach out your hand and put it into my side" (John 20:27). Confronted with tangible proof, Thomas fell on his knees exclaiming, "My Lord and my God!" (John 20:28). Jesus affirmed Thomas's faith, blessing those who would believe without seeing (John 20:29). This encounter illustrates that resurrection faith embraces both the testimony of others and, at times, the longing for personal assurance.

Thomas's journey from skepticism to confession models the interplay between doubt and faith in the Christian life. His honest demand for evidence resonates with seekers who wrestle with unseen realities. Yet Jesus' response—appearing despite Thomas's absence and offering the very proofs he requested—reveals divine patience and respect for human questioning. The Lord's blessing on future believers without sight ("blessed are those who have not seen and yet have believed") broadens the scope of genuine faith (John 20:29). Thomas's experience encourages all readers to bring their uncertainties before Christ, trusting that He meets our doubts with presence, revelation, and grace.

4.1.3 Peter's Restoration by the Sea

After the resurrection, several disciples returned to their former occupation of fishing on the Sea of Tiberias, perhaps seeking solace in familiarity (John 21:1). At dawn, they caught nothing until a stranger on the shore instructed them to cast the net on the right side of the boat, resulting in a miraculous haul of 153 fish (John 21:6). Recognizing the Lord, John signaled Peter, who impulsively plunged into the water to greet Him (John 21:7). Ashore, Jesus prepared a charcoal fire with fish and bread, echoing Peter's own denial beside a charcoal fire days earlier (cf. Luke 22:56–62). After they ate, Jesus asked Peter three times, "Do you love me?" Each affirmation of love corresponded to one of Peter's denials, and each time Jesus commissioned him, "Feed my lambs...tend my sheep...feed my sheep" (John 21:15–17). Peter's restoration underscores that resurrection grace not only forgives failure but also restores purpose and leadership.

This seaside encounter weaves together themes of failure, forgiveness, and fruitful ministry. Peter's earlier brash denials gave way to humble confessions and renewed vocation. The number three—a biblical symbol of completeness—marks both Peter's failure and his reinstatement. By entrusting shepherding responsibilities to Peter, Jesus affirmed the continuity of apostolic authority grounded in resurrection life. Furthermore, the meal on the beach transforms labor into fellowship, reminding believers that everyday work can be animated by risen presence. Peter's reintegration into community and mission exemplifies how resurrected relationships recalibrate identity and calling.

4.1.4 An Appearance to James

Among the post-resurrection appearances catalogued by Paul in 1 Corinthians 15:3–8 is a brief note that Jesus "appeared to James." James, the half-brother of Jesus, had been a skeptic during His earthly ministry (John 7:5). Yet after encountering the risen Lord, James emerged as a pillar of the Jerusalem church (Galatians 2:9), leading the Council of Jerusalem and authoring a letter that echoes Jesus' ethical teachings. This personal appearance bridged familial distance, transforming James from doubt to devotion. The significance of Christ's appearance to His own brother lies in the restoration of family bonds and the empowerment of leadership across relational divides. In experiencing resurrection firsthand, James personifies how the risen Lord appoints unexpected witnesses to advance the gospel in diverse contexts.

James's example also highlights the breadth of resurrection witness. The risen Christ did not limit appearances to His closest disciples but extended personal encounters to those on the margins of belief—even within His own family. James's transformation underscores that no background or prior skepticism disqualifies one from resurrection encounter and mission. His subsequent influence in reconciling Jewish and Gentile believers speaks to the unifying power of the risen

Lord. Thus, the appearance to James testifies to resurrection's capacity to reshape relationships and to commission leaders regardless of their past positions or presuppositions.

4.1.5 Saul's Damascus Road Encounter

Perhaps the most dramatic individual appearance is Jesus' revelation to Saul of Tarsus on the road to Damascus (Acts 9:1–9). As a zealous persecutor of the church, Saul encountered a blinding light and heard the voice, "Saul, Saul, why do you persecute me?" (Acts 9:4). Struck mute and blind, he was led into Damascus, where Ananias—acting on divine direction—laid hands on him, restoring sight and baptizing him (Acts 9:17–18). Saul's transformation into Paul the apostle exemplifies resurrection power breaking through religious zealotry to create new identity and mission. In addressing persecution of the church as personal offense against Christ, the encounter reveals the mystical union between Christ and His body. Paul's subsequent ministry to the Gentiles— grounded in the reality of resurrection—demonstrates how an appearance can redirect life's course toward world-embracing proclamation.

The Damascus road event also underscores that resurrection encounters can occur beyond physical proximity to the tomb. Jesus appears to Saul in brightness and voice, without bodily form, yet the impact is life-changing. This meeting introduces the theme of the risen Lord revealing Himself in unexpected ways, often to those least likely to receive grace. Paul's testimony, immediately shared across synagogues and churches, became a cornerstone of early Christian identity. His conversion story continues to encourage seekers, reminding us that resurrection life breaks into human hearts wherever Jesus wills, forging apostolic ministry from the most unlikely candidates.

4.2 Small-Group Encounters

4.2.1 Two Disciples on the Road to Emmaus

Luke recounts how two disciples journeyed to the village of Emmaus, discussing recent events with downcast hearts (Luke 24:13–14). Unrecognized, Jesus joined them and asked, "What is this conversation that you are holding with each other as you walk?" (Luke 24:17). They explained their dashed hopes and confusion over the empty tomb and reports of angels and visions of Jesus alive. Beginning with Moses and all the Prophets, He interpreted the Scriptures concerning Himself, unveiling the necessity of suffering and glory (Luke 24:27). As they reached Emmaus, they urged Him to stay, and at the table, He took bread, blessed and broke it, and gave it to them—then their eyes were opened (Luke 24:30–31). In that instant, He vanished, leaving them to exclaim, "Did not our hearts burn within us while he talked to us on the road?" (Luke 24:32). Their immediate return to Jerusalem to share the good news models how Word and sacrament work together to reveal the risen Lord and kindle mission.

This Emmaus encounter emphasizes that resurrection revelation unfolds through dialogue with Scripture and shared meal. The pattern of journey, dialogue, recognition, and commissioning provides a template for discipleship that endures to this day. The disciples moved from confusion to conviction, illustrating how Jesus opens minds to understand prophetic testimony when hearts are inclined toward Him. Their burning hearts testify that spiritual illumination often involves a felt sense of warmth and urgency. By recounting this story, Luke invites readers to emulate the Emmaus road pattern: engage Scripture, break bread, recognize Christ's presence, and hasten to bear witness.

4.2.2 Eleven in the Upper Room

Late on resurrection evening, the eleven disciples gathered behind locked doors in fear of Jewish authorities (Luke 24:36). Suddenly, Jesus stood among them and greeted them with the peace of God: "Peace be with you" (Luke 24:36). They were startled and frightened, thinking they saw a spirit, until He showed them His hands and feet, inviting them to touch and see that "a spirit does not have flesh and bones as you see that I have" (Luke 24:39). To further dispel doubt, He asked for and ate a piece of broiled fish (Luke 24:41–43). Through this shared meal, He affirmed His bodily resurrection and bridged the disciples' past experiences of fellowship and fellowship anticipating future mission. This encounter inaugurates communal fellowship with the risen Lord as the basis for church life. It signals that resurrection is not a private event but a corporate reality meant to be celebrated in community.

The locked doors underscore both the disciples' fear and the new quality of Jesus' risen body—transcending physical barriers. His greeting of peace, echoing Isaiah's promise of shalom (Isaiah 52:7), situates resurrection as the foundation for reconciliation. By eating with them, Jesus sanctified the material creation, affirming that resurrection life embraces the physical realm. The Upper Room meeting thus provides the archetype for Christian worship: Word, peace-greeting, and shared meal within the gathered community. It also foreshadows the Eucharistic celebration, where believers encounter the risen Lord and receive the peace He grants.

4.2.3 Eleven with Thomas Present

On the subsequent evening, Jesus again appeared to the disciples in the locked room, this time with Thomas present (John 20:19–23). He greeted them, "Peace be with you," and then "breathed on them, and said to them, 'Receive the Holy Spirit'" (John 20:22). This breath gesture recalls God's creative breath in Genesis ("the breath of life") and signals new-creation reality inaugurated by resurrection. Jesus then commissioned them to forgive sins, granting authority rooted in His atonement (John 20:23). Thomas's presence—once absent—now complete, underscores communal reconciliation and shared mission. The appearance affirms that resurrection life brings peace, empowerment, and purpose for the community charged with continuing Christ's ministry. It establishes the linkage between resurrection and Spirit-endowment that fuels the church's witness.

This gathering highlights how resurrection encounters prepare the disciples for mission. The impartation of the Spirit before Pentecost indicates that Jesus' resurrection and ascension inaugurate new covenant blessings. Granting authority to forgive sins situates the church as agent of reconciliation in the world, empowered by resurrection life. The communal nature of the encounter builds unity among the disciples, reinforcing that mission flows from shared experience of Christ's presence. Thomas, once skeptical, now participates fully, exemplifying how resurrection transforms community members and sustains collective witness.

4.2.4 Seven Disciples by the Sea

John's Gospel also narrates a third appearance by the Sea of Galilee, where seven disciples fished without success until Jesus appeared on the shore and instructed them to cast the net on the right side (John 21:3–6). The miraculous catch of 153 fish awed them, and John recognized Jesus before Peter hurried into the water (John 21:7). On shore, Jesus had prepared bread and fish over a charcoal fire, echoing epiphanies of provision and fellowship (John 21:9). This setting recalls Peter's denial by a charcoal fire, now transformed into an occasion of restoration and provision (John 21:9; Luke 22:56). After breakfast, Jesus thrice asked Peter, "Do you love me?" linking each confession to a pastoral commission (John 21:15–17). The seven disciples' gathering dramatizes how resurrection invites disciples back into vocation, fellowship, and leadership under Christ's compassionate gaze.

This appearance reinforces themes of restoration and mission within the rhythms of daily life. By choosing a familiar setting of fishing, Jesus met the disciples where they were, blending the ordinary with the extraordinary. The beach-side meal becomes a microcosm of kingdom life, where work, word, and worship converge. Peter's reinstatement underscores that resurrection transforms failure into commissioning. The number seven—symbolic of completeness—frames this group as representative of the church set to be "fishers of men" (Mark 1:17). Thus, the Sea of Galilee encounter models how resurrection shapes both identity and vocation in community.

4.2.5 Eleven on the Mountain in Galilee

Matthew concludes his Gospel with the disciples meeting Jesus on a mountain in Galilee, where He had directed them (Matthew 28:16–17). Upon seeing Him, some worshiped while others doubted, reflecting authentic faith amid hesitation. Jesus approached and declared, "All authority in heaven and on earth has been given to me" (Matthew 28:18). He then commissioned them to make disciples of all nations, baptizing and teaching them to obey everything He commanded (Matthew 28:19–20). The mountain motif echoes Sinai and Transfiguration scenes, signifying divine revelation and covenant renewal. The Great Commission's trinitarian baptismal formula roots mission in the fullness of God's identity. This climactic encounter connects resurrection authority with global mission, assuring the church of Christ's ongoing presence: "I am with you always, to the end of the age."

Here, the blend of worship and doubt acknowledges that resurrection encounter does not obliterate human uncertainty but invites worshiping faith even in the midst of questions. The mountain setting situates mission within the context of divine encounter, highlighting that obedience flows from revelation. The trinitarian commissioning unites the church's activity with the life of the triune God. By promising His abiding presence, Jesus links resurrection vindication with perpetual companionship. The mountain scene thus encapsulates how personal encounter leads to corporate mission under the risen Lord's sovereign authority.

4.3 Public Proclamations & Final Commissions

4.3.1 The Great Commission

In the wake of resurrection appearances, Jesus entrusted His followers with a universal mandate: to make disciples of all nations, baptizing them into the triune name and teaching them to obey His commands (Matthew 28:18–20). This instruction rests on the bedrock of resurrection authority: "All authority in heaven and on earth has been given to me" (v. 18). The triadic baptismal formula signals that new life in the Spirit is integral to the church's identity and mission. The call to teach obedience to Christ's commands links formation with discipleship, ensuring that knowledge of resurrection translates into transformed living. The promise "I am with you always" anchors the task in the constancy of His presence. By commissioning both Apostles and future disciples, Jesus ensures that resurrection witness extends beyond an initial generation.

The Great Commission also echoes Old Testament mission themes: God's intention to bless all nations through Abraham's seed (Genesis 12:3) and the prophetic vision of nations streaming to Zion (Isaiah 2:2–4). Jesus positions the church as the conduit of this blessing, empowered by resurrection authority. The emphasis on teaching underscores that mission involves both proclamation and character formation. The global scope—"to the ends of the earth"—signals that no culture or people group lies outside resurrection's ken. In sum, the Great Commission situates personal encounters with the risen Lord within a grand, continuous narrative of God's redemptive purposes for the world.

4.3.2 The Forty-Day Ministry in Jerusalem

Luke records that Jesus presented Himself alive over a period of forty days, speaking about the kingdom of God (Acts 1:3). This extended ministry allowed the disciples to transition from seared grief to mature faith, grounding their witness in sustained interaction with the risen Lord. During these weeks,

He offered teaching, encouragement, and correction, preparing them for the outpouring of the Holy Spirit. The forty-day motif recalls Israel's wilderness trials and Moses' encounters, signifying a season of testing and formation. By appearing repeatedly, Jesus validated their testimonies and deepened their understanding of kingdom dynamics. This period culminated in the ascension, ensuring that the church's mission would proceed under both resurrected and ascended leadership. The forty-day ministry thus bridges the gap between resurrection revelation and Pentecostal commissioning.

Luke's emphasis on "many convincing proofs" (Acts 1:3) underscores that resurrection ministry was anchored in evidence and experiential authenticity. The period allowed the disciples to wrestle with theological implications—such as the relationship between death, resurrection, and eschatological reign. Their sustained proximity to Jesus in Jerusalem fostered unity and anticipation, setting the stage for the birth of the church at Pentecost. Moreover, by focusing on the kingdom of God, Jesus linked resurrection victory with present and future reality, shaping the church's vision of God's reign. The forty-day ministry reminds believers that resurrection encounter ignites both worship and preparedness for Spirit-empowered mission.

4.3.3 Promise of the Holy Spirit

Prior to His ascension, Jesus instructed the disciples to remain in Jerusalem until they were baptized with the Holy Spirit (Acts 1:4–5). This promise, reiterated by John the Baptist and Jesus Himself, connected resurrection to Spirit-empowerment (Luke 3:16; John 7:39). On the day of Pentecost, this outpouring inaugurated the church's mission with miraculous signs, bold proclamation, and global momentum (Acts 2:1–4). The Spirit's descent fulfilled Old Testament promises (Joel 2:28–29), equipping the community to bear witness to Jesus' resurrection across linguistic and cultural barriers. The resurrection-Spirit nexus demonstrates that new life in Christ involves transformation from within, enabling the church to reflect Christ's character and power. By promising the Spirit, Jesus ensured that resurrection encounter would be accompanied by divine presence and gifting for ongoing ministry.

The promise also underscores that resurrection and Pentecost are inseparable chapters of the same redemptive work. While the empty tomb vindicates Christ's identity, the Spirit's outpouring advances His mission through empowered witnesses. The Spirit's role in convicting the world of sin, righteousness, and judgment (John 16:8) arises directly from Christ's ascent and resurrection. This dynamic reveals that resurrection life is both vertical—reconciled to the Father—and horizontal—sent into the world with divine authority. The promised Spirit thus becomes the present reality of the risen Lord dwelling within the church, ensuring His ongoing activity among mankind.

4.3.4 The Ascension at Bethany

Luke and Acts describe Jesus leading the disciples to Bethany, blessing them, and then being lifted up into heaven as a cloud received Him (Luke 24:50–51; Acts 1:9). The ascension marks the culmination of resurrection appearances and the beginning of Jesus' exalted ministry as High Priest and intercessor (Hebrews 7:25). The cloud imagery echoes Old Testament theophanies, affirming that the ascended Christ sits at the right hand of God (Psalm 110:1). The angels' promise that He will return in the same manner (Acts 1:11) fixes the church's hope on His second coming. The disciples' subsequent worship and joy (Luke 24:52) model the appropriate response to ascending glory. The ascension thus completes the resurrection-exaltation cycle, commissioning the church under heavenly leadership while anticipating Christ's return.

Through the ascension, Jesus transitions from embodied presence to Spirit-mediated presence, sending the Comforter while inaugurating a new form of union with believers. His enthronement secures the church's access to the Father, shaping its theology of prayer and intercession. The promise of return instills urgency in mission and perseverance in suffering. By blessing His followers before departure, Jesus affirms that resurrection commissioning extends beyond earthly appearances into eternal reality. The ascension, therefore, anchors the church's identity as a resurrection community living under the reign of an exalted Lord.

4.4 Themes & Patterns in Risen Encounters

4.4.1 Physicality of the Resurrection Body

A consistent theme in resurrection appearances is the physicality of Jesus' body. He invites Thomas to touch His wounds (John 20:27) and encourages the disciples to handle Him and see Him, for "a spirit does not have flesh and bones as you see that I have" (Luke 24:39). He eats broiled fish and honeycomb (Luke 24:42–43; John 21:9–13), demonstrating that resurrection life is not ghostly but embodied. The nail marks and pierced side become perpetual proofs of the continuity between crucifixion and resurrection, underlining that Jesus truly died and rose again. This corporeal reality counters docetic notions that the resurrection was purely spiritual illusion. The physical resurrection body foreshadows the future glorified bodies believers will receive (1 Corinthians 15:42–44). The incarnational pattern affirms the goodness of creation, setting the stage for Christian hope in bodily renewal.

By grounding resurrection in physicality, the Gospel narratives protect against any drift toward dualistic contempt for the material world. Jesus' post-resurrection meals and wounds underscore that salvation involves the whole person—body and soul. The physicality of His appearances also legitimates sacramental practices like Eucharist and baptism, which employ tangible elements to convey spiritual realities. In emphasizing the real, bodily presence of the risen Lord, Scripture assures believers that God's redemption extends to the fullness of creation, not merely to disembodied souls.

4.4.2 Recognition and Revelation

Many resurrection encounters follow a pattern of initial non-recognition followed by revelatory disclosure. Mary mistakes

Jesus for the gardener until He speaks her name (John 20:14–16). The Emmaus disciples fail to recognize Him until He breaks bread (Luke 24:30–31). This motif teaches that resurrected presence may be hidden until the familiar rhythms of fellowship and worship awaken recognition. Such patterns remind believers that spiritual sight often requires participation in Word and sacrament. Similarly, Jesus opens the Scriptures to the Emmaus pair, revealing that prophecy points to His suffering and glory (Luke 24:27). Recognition thus combines relational familiarity, liturgical action, and Scriptural illumination. These episodes encourage contemporary disciples to cultivate attentiveness to Christ's subtle presence in communal worship, Scripture reading, and shared meal.

Recognition also often leads to worship: the women "took hold of his feet and worshiped him" (Matthew 28:9); the Emmaus disciples "rose that same hour and returned to Jerusalem" with hearts burning (Luke 24:32). Revelation transforms confusion into conviction, prompting mission. The consistent sequence—hidden presence, revelatory act, obedient response—provides a template for faith formation. It asserts that encounter with the risen Lord is both objective (He is present) and experiential (we perceive Him). Understanding this pattern equips believers to seek and recognize Jesus in varied contexts today.

4.4.3 Commissioning and Sending

Resurrection encounters invariably transition into commissioning. Mary is sent to tell the disciples (John 20:17–18); Peter is charged to feed Christ's sheep (John 21:15–17); the eleven receive the Great Commission (Matthew 28:19–20); the disciples are empowered to forgive sins (John 20:23); Paul is called to missionary enterprise (Acts 9:15). These directives link personal encounter with communal mission. The risen Lord entrusts His followers with tasks that flow from His victory over sin and death. Commissioning affirms that resurrection is not merely for individual blessing but for corporate witness. Each command carries the authority of the risen Christ and the promise of His presence. The sending impulse seeded in these appearances structures the church's identity: an apostolic community sent into the world under Christ's resurrected lordship.

The variety of commissions—proclamation, pastoral care, sacramental authority, global mission—demonstrates the breadth of resurrection-empowered service. Women, fishermen, insiders, outsiders all receive assignments, indicating that every follower has a role. By rooting commissioning in encounter, Scripture underscores that mission arises from intimacy with the risen Lord rather than human strategy. This encounter-mission dynamic remains vital for empowering contemporary disciples to bear witness in word and deed.

4.4.4 Fulfillment of Scripture and Promise

Throughout the post-resurrection narratives, Jesus and His followers highlight how appearances fulfill Scripture and prior promises. Luke emphasizes that Christ opened the Law, Prophets, and Psalms concerning Himself (Luke 24:27,44). Peter's Pentecost sermon cites Psalm 16 to explain David's prophecy of resurrection (Acts 2:29–32). Paul in Corinth recites creedal tradition that Christ was raised "according to the Scriptures" (1 Corinthians 15:3–4). Emmaus disciples recall how Scripture foretold Messiah's suffering and glory (Luke 24:26–27). These references forge a seamless continuity between Old Testament hope and New Testament fulfillment. Resurrection appearances thus serve as the divine "amen" to prophetic promises, anchoring Christian faith in the reliability of God's Word. They assure believers that resurrection life is not an isolated miracle but the apex of God's covenantal narrative.

By underscoring fulfillment, the Gospel writers combat any notion that Jesus' rising was an unanticipated afterthought. Instead, they frame it as the culmination of redemptive history foretold from Eden onward—Jonah's three days in the fish (Matthew 12:40), David's trust in not seeing decay (Acts 2:25–28), the Suffering Servant's vindication (Isaiah 53). The consistent theme of fulfillment invites readers to read Scripture Christocentrically, seeing all of Scripture converging in the resurrection. This hermeneutical key shapes theology, preaching, and devotion, ensuring that resurrection remains the lens through which all biblical revelation is interpreted.

4.5 Encounter as Foundation for the Church Today

4.5.1 Worship Rooted in Easter Encounter

The early church's worship life emerged directly from resurrection encounters: the Lord's Supper commemorates both crucifixion and resurrection (1 Corinthians 11:23–26), while Easter liturgies dramatize the empty tomb and Christ's appearances. Hymns like the ancient Exsultet or "Christ the Lord Is Risen Today" retell resurrection narratives, inviting congregations into the first-century astonishment. Church architecture—orienting altars eastward—symbolizes rising sun and rising Savior. Even the use of Easter candle and paschal candle ritual recapitulates themes of light overcoming darkness, echoing the Emmaus road's "burning hearts" and Mary's dawning recognition. By rooting worship in resurrection story and encounter motifs, the church perpetuates first-hand testimonies across generations.

This resurrection-shaped worship also features readings that cycle annually through Gospel appearances (the lectionary's Easter season), ensuring that congregations regularly hear narratives of Christ's risen presence. Liturgical gestures—like the peace greeting—recreate His first words to the fearful disciples (Luke 24:36). Through music, proclamation, sacrament, and symbol, Christian worship remains a space of ongoing encounter with the risen Lord. Such worship not only remembers the past but mediates present experience of resurrection power, sustaining faith amid the challenges of today.

4.5.2 Discipleship through Encounter

Contemporary discipleship programs often mirror Emmaus-style patterns: small groups meet to break bread, discuss Scripture, and share experiences of Christ's presence. Retreats and spiritual formation communities adopt pilgrimage or "road" models, guiding participants through stages of confusion, revelation, and commissioning. Personal devotions echo Mary's solitary vigil at the tomb, encouraging seekers to linger in prayer until Christ reveals Himself. The practice of lectio divina—slow, prayerful reading of Scripture—recreates the disciples' experience of Jesus opening the Scriptures on the road (Luke 24:32). Encounter-centered discipleship emphasizes that growth in Christ arises not merely from information but from relational revelation and communal practice. By integrating Word, sacrament, and fellowship, believers find their own hearts "burning" with truth.

Prioritizing encounter also safeguards against merely programmatic approaches to faith. When discipleship centers on personal and communal encounters with the risen Lord, it yields authentic transformation rather than superficial compliance. It trains believers to recognize Christ's presence amid life's journeys and equips them to respond with worship and obedience. By following models from early post-resurrection gatherings—locked-door fellowship, seaside meals, mountain-top commissioning—churches today can foster environments where resurrection reality is encountered and lived out.

4.5.3 Mission Modeled on Apostolic Sending

The apostolic pattern established by resurrection appearances—encounter, commission, sending—continues to shape missional engagement. Cross-cultural missionaries echo Paul's Damascus road conversion, testifying that resurrection can transform hostility into service. Church planting movements adopt the Great Commission's trinitarian baptismal mandate, contextualizing Scripture and practice for every culture. Evangelistic efforts mirror Mary's announcement to the disciples: personal testimony based on authentic encounter. Compassion ministries reflect Jesus' shepherding commands—feeding sheep through acts of mercy. The synergy of encounter and mission assures that outreach flows from personal conviction rather than programmatic pressure. Resurrection encounter thus remains the primary catalyst for global mission, empowering believers to "go and make disciples."

Moreover, mission strategies grounded in resurrection embrace both proclamation and demonstration of kingdom life—balancing Word and deed as expressions of the risen Christ's compassion. Just as Jesus appeared on roads, in rooms, by the sea, and on mountains, mission takes place in diverse contexts, shaped by local culture and need. By heeding the apostolic example, contemporary churches maintain fidelity to the mission profile inaugurated by resurrection.

4.5.4 Living in Hope of Future Encounters

Resurrection appearances conclude with ascension and promise of return, anchoring Christian hope in future consummation. Just as the disciples witnessed resurrection and ascension, believers live in anticipation of Christ's second coming (Acts 1:11). This eschatological horizon influences ethics, worship, and mission, infusing life with purpose and perseverance. When churches recite the Apostles' Creed— "He ascended into heaven...He will come again to judge the living and the dead"—they reaffirm hope grounded in historical resurrection and promised return. Such hope sustains faith amid trials, encouraging believers to persevere as those who have already encountered the risen Lord and await His final appearing.

Living in hope also shapes communal identity: the church as a "field hospital" (Bonhoeffer) ministering in anticipation of full healing, a "colony of heaven" embodying resurrection virtues in the present, and a "harbinger of glory" pointing toward the new heavens and new earth (Revelation 21:1). By centering life on the promise of future encounter, the church remains both missionary and pilgrim, grounded in resurrection history and anticipating its fulfillment. Thus, the pattern of encounter extends beyond the past into a living, forward-looking hope that propels every aspect of Christian existence.

Conclusion The manifold appearances of Jesus after His resurrection form the lifeblood of Christian faith and practice. In solitary encounters and corporate gatherings, by the tomb, on the road, beside the lake, and on a mountain, the risen Lord revealed Himself in ways that healed wounds, ignited mission, and deepened worship. Through touch, word, meal, and breath, He confirmed the continuity of His incarnation and inaugurated the new reality of resurrection life empowered by the Spirit. These encounters not only vindicate Christ's identity but also establish patterns—recognition, commissioning, sending—that shape the church's worship, discipleship, and mission across centuries. As contemporary followers retrace these steps through Scripture, sacrament, and communal life, we join the original witnesses in testifying that death has lost its dominion and life has triumphed. May our own experiences of the risen Lord continue to renew our hope, embolden our witness, and unite us in the shared journey toward His promised return.

Chapter 5: Theological Foundations—Why the Resurrection Matters

The resurrection of Jesus Christ stands at the very heart of Christian theology, serving as the pivotal event that validates everything He taught and accomplished. Without the resurrection, the cross risks being perceived as a tragic defeat rather than the decisive victory over sin, death, and evil powers. In His rising, Christ secures the believer's justification, inaugurates a new creation, and guarantees the ultimate restoration of all things. This chapter explores the foundational doctrines that flow from Easter morning, tracing how resurrection life reshapes the believer's identity, hope, ethics, and mission. Drawing on key New Testament passages— from Pauline epistles to Johannine narratives—we will examine why the resurrection matters not only as historical fact but as the wellspring of transformative power for individuals, the church, and society at large. Whether confronting personal guilt, facing trials, or envisioning the world to come, Christians ground their confidence in the reality that Christ is risen indeed. As we unpack these theological truths, may our own faith be deepened and our worship enriched by the truth that resurrection life is our present possession and future hope.

5.1 Victory Over Sin and Death

The resurrection of Jesus signals the decisive overthrow of sin's sovereignty and death's sting. In rising, Christ demonstrates that the grave no longer serves as humanity's final frontier, but rather as the threshold into new life. This victory is not merely symbolic; it impacts believers at the deepest levels by reconciling them to God, empowering them against spiritual enemies, and redeemer life in a world marred by corruption. By uniting death and resurrection in a single salvific act, Scripture teaches that believers share in both events—dying to sin and rising to righteousness. This chapter's first section examines how union with Christ, cosmic conquest over demonic powers, and the legal declarations of justification rest squarely on the reality of Easter morning.

5.1.1 Union with Christ in His Death and Resurrection

Paul unfolds the doctrine of union with Christ in Romans 6:3–5, explaining that through baptism believers are "buried with him by baptism into death" so that "just as Christ was raised from the dead... we too might walk in newness of life." This mystical solidarity means that when Christ died, believers died with Him to the reign of sin; when He rose, they too rose to participate in His righteousness. The imagery of burial followed by resurrection underscores that the cross and the empty tomb are inseparable components of redemption. It is in this union that deliverance from sin's power occurs—not through moral effort alone but through incorporation into Christ's victorious death and life. Union with Christ also grounds the believer's new identity "in Him" (Galatians 2:20), assuring that the old self has been crucified and the new self empowered by the risen Lord. This union both liberates from sin's domination (Romans 6:6) and establishes a continual trajectory of transformation, as the believer progressively manifests resurrection life in sanctified living.

5.1.2 Defeat of Satan and Demonic Powers

Colossians 2:15 proclaims that Christ "disarmed the rulers and authorities and put them to open shame, by triumphing over them in him," indicating that the resurrection was the public demonstration of Christ's authority over all spiritual adversaries. Likewise, Hebrews 2:14–15 explains that Jesus shared in flesh and blood "that through death he might destroy the one who has the power of death, that is, the devil," freeing humanity from the fear of death that Satan wields. Resurrection, therefore, serves as the decisive blow against demonic dominion; it invalidates the devil's claim to existential authority. Believers, united to the risen Christ, participate in this victory (1 John 4:4), assured that no demonic scheme can reverse resurrection triumph. This cosmic scope of conquest invites the church to engage in spiritual warfare with confidence—prayer, proclamation, and sacramental life draw upon resurrection power to resist evil. The cross broke sin's claim; the empty tomb shatters Satan's stronghold, vindicating God's plan to restore creation.

5.1.3 Justification and Redemption

In Romans 4:25, Paul ties resurrection directly to justification: "He was delivered up for our trespasses and raised for our justification." The empty tomb thus functions as God's legal declaration of acquittal—death's roar is silenced and sin's verdict overturned. Peter echoes this in 1 Peter 1:3–5, emphasizing a "new birth into a living hope through the resurrection of Jesus Christ from the dead," which secures an inheritance imperishable and undefiled. Justification, the forensic act by which God pardons sinners, finds its definitive proof in Christ's rising: death could not hold the righteous One, affirming the sufficiency of His atoning sacrifice. Simultaneously, redemption—the act of purchasing back slaves from bondage—occurs as resurrection power rescues believers from sin's enslaving grip. This dual reality shapes how Christians relate to God: they stand righteous before Him by faith in the risen Christ and enjoy restored relationship, no longer estranged by sin. Resurrection life thus undergirds the believer's reconciled standing and ongoing experience of redemption.

5.2 Assurance of Salvation and Hope

Resurrection also provides the bedrock for Christian assurance and living hope amid life's uncertainties. Because Christ has risen, believers can know with certainty that their salvation is irreversible and their future secure. This section explores how Christ's firstfruits guarantee, the hope born from suffering, and the Spirit's witness to sonship converge to produce an unwavering confidence in the believer's eternal destiny. In a world riddled with doubt and despair, resurrection hope becomes an anchor for the soul, sustaining joy and perseverance.

5.2.1 Firstfruits of Resurrection (1 Corinthians 15:20)

Paul describes Christ as "the firstfruits of those who have fallen asleep" (1 Corinthians 15:20), employing the Old Testament practice of offering the first portion of the harvest as a guarantee of the full crop to follow (Leviticus 23:10–11). Likewise, Christ's resurrection serves as the down payment (arrabōn, Ephesians 1:14) of the general resurrection that awaits believers. The pattern is clear: the risen Lord pries open eternity, assuring us that individual resurrection will follow. This firstfruits motif provides a firm basis for hope rooted not in wishful thinking but in the historical and cosmic reality of Christ's own rise. Believers, therefore, live in the tension of "already" assured resurrection life and "not yet" fully realized redemption of body and creation. This guarantee fosters confidence that death's sting is taken away and that future bodily transformation is as certain as Christ's own.

5.2.2 Living Hope Through Suffering (1 Peter 1:3–9)

Peter emphasizes that Christians have been "born again to a living hope through the resurrection of Jesus Christ from the dead" (1 Peter 1:3). Even amid trials that test faith like fire, this living hope sustains believers in joy "inexpressible and filled with glory" (v. 8). Whereas suffering often erodes hope in the world, resurrection provides an ultimate perspective: pain is temporary, suffering refines faith, and glory awaits. The reality of Christ's rising compels believers to view hardship not as abandonment but as part of redemptive training (Romans 5:3–5). Early martyrs bore witness to this hope, facing death with courage because they trusted in resurrection vindication. Pastoral ministries draw from this reservoir of hope, encouraging the afflicted that resurrection life transcends present darkness. In sum, living hope transforms suffering into sanctifying opportunity, anchoring the soul when circumstances rage.

5.2.3 Security in Sonship (Romans 8:16–17)

Paul further links resurrection to the believer's identity as a child of God: "The Spirit himself bears witness with our spirit that we are children of God" (Romans 8:16). Resurrection life is inseparable from adoption—believers become heirs of God and co-heirs with Christ (v. 17). This adoption underwrites a confidence that believers no longer stand condemned (Romans 8:1) but enjoy full filial privileges. The Spirit's inner testimony assures perseverance: even when self-doubt or external accusations arise, the Spirit affirms resurrection reality in the heart. Thus, resurrection and adoption coalesce to form an unshakeable foundation for assurance, quelling existential anxieties. This security flows into discipleship, freeing believers to serve and love without fear of abandonment. As sons and daughters, Christians live boldly, knowing that resurrection unity with Christ guarantees their eternal inheritance and divine presence.

5.3 Sanctification and New Life

Beyond personal assurance, resurrection life propels believers into ongoing transformation—sanctification. The same power that raised Christ from the dead energizes new-creation living, enabling moral renewal and ethical vitality. As the Spirit indwells and conforms believers to Christ's image, resurrection becomes the engine for holiness. This section examines how the indwelling Spirit, resurrection-informed ethics, and the dynamic of mortification and vivification shape Christian growth.

5.3.1 Indwelling Spirit and Resurrection Power (Ephesians 1:19–20)

Paul prays that believers would grasp "what is the immeasurable greatness of his power toward us who believe…which he exerted in Christ when he raised him from the dead" (Ephesians 1:19–20). That same power now dwells in believers by the Holy Spirit (Romans 8:11), enabling them to live above sin's pull. Sanctification thus flows from Spirit-empowered union with the risen Lord—resurrection life is not self-generated but imparted. This divine enablement transforms affections and actions, leading to the fruit of the Spirit (Galatians 5:22–23). Recognizing sanctification as participation in resurrection power fosters humility and dependence on God, rather than mere moral striving. Spiritual disciplines—prayer, Scripture meditation, community— become conduits for resurrection life, cultivating Christlike character. Therefore, holiness emerges not from religious effort alone but from the Spirit's resurrecting work in the believer's heart.

5.3.2 New Creation Ethics (Colossians 3:1–17)

Colossians 3:1–17 presents a programmatic ethic for those "who have been raised with Christ." Believers are instructed to "set your minds on things that are above" (v. 2), to put off the old self with its vices and to "put on the new self, which is being renewed in knowledge after the image of its creator" (vv. 9–10). This ethical transformation flows directly from resurrection reality, as new creation living replaces former patterns. Compassion, kindness, humility, patience, forgiveness, and love shape interpersonal relations, reflecting the life of the risen Lord. Marital, familial, and communal ethics find their anchor in Christ's reconciliation brought about through resurrection. By situating moral exhortation within resurrection context, Paul ensures that ethical life is not optional addendum but the necessary fruit of new life. Thus, resurrection refashions community, creating an environment where grace and righteousness flourish together.

5.3.3 Progressive Mortification and Vivification (Romans 8:13)

Paul admonishes believers to put to death "the deeds of the body" by the Spirit, knowing that those who live according to the Spirit "will put to death the deeds of the body and live" (Romans 8:13). This interplay of mortification (dying to sin) and vivification (living by the Spirit) mirrors the death–resurrection pattern of Christ. Mortification involves active resistance to sin—turning away from former behaviors—while vivification emphasizes dependence on resurrected life to bear spiritual fruit. Over time, this dynamic process deepens Christlikeness, as believers increasingly experience the life-giving power of resurrection in practical holiness. Spiritual disciplines support mortification and vivification, providing frameworks for cooperative transformation. Recognizing sanctification as a resurrection-empowered journey alleviates legalism and fosters enduring growth. In this way, resurrection theology underwrites both the victory over sin and the ongoing pursuit of holiness.

5.4 Eschatological Fulfillment

The resurrection also serves as the inaugural act of final redemption, inaugurating the kingdom of God and guaranteeing the future resurrection of the body. Christian eschatology pivots on Christ's rising as the firstfruits of a cosmic harvest that will culminate in the renewal of creation and final judgment. This section examines how resurrection shapes beliefs about bodily resurrection, kingdom consummation, and eternal life in both blessing and judgment.

5.4.1 Resurrection of the Body (1 Corinthians 15:35–58)

Paul addresses skeptics in Corinth by defending the reality and nature of the resurrection body (1 Corinthians 15:35–58). He contrasts "natural" bodies subject to decay with "spiritual" bodies imperishable and glorious (vv. 42–44). Christ's resurrection body provides the prototype: though He bore marks of crucifixion, He possessed new qualities—transcending tomb and time. Believers who are "in Christ" will likewise receive transformed bodies suited for eternal life (v. 53). This doctrine affirms the value of bodily existence and counters dualistic contempt for the material world. The certainty of bodily resurrection sustains ethical care for the body—opposing abortion, euthanasia, and neglect. Paul concludes with triumphant faith: "Death is swallowed up in victory" (v. 54), and "thanks be to God, who gives us the victory through our Lord Jesus Christ" (v. 57). Resurrection of the body thus shapes the church's hope, ethics, and dignity accorded to human life.

5.4.2 Inauguration of the Kingdom (Acts 2:32–36)

Peter's sermon at Pentecost anchors the inauguration of God's kingdom firmly in resurrected Christ: "God has made him both Lord and Christ...this Jesus whom you crucified" (Acts 2:36). Resurrection is portrayed as enthronement, ushering in the kingdom that had been foretold by the prophets. Yet this kingdom is "already" present in the church's life and mission while "not yet" fully consummated until Christ returns. This tension energizes the church's witness, pressing toward justice, peace, and righteousness. Signs and wonders accompany apostolic proclamation (Acts 4:29–31), signaling kingdom authority over sickness and demonic forces. Resurrection thus serves as the hinge between the now and the not yet, empowering believers to live as citizens of heaven while awaiting consummation. The inaugurated kingdom motivates missional engagement, social renewal, and spiritual formation in light of Christ's reign.

5.4.3 Final Judgment and Eternal Life (John 5:28–29; Revelation 20:4–6)

Jesus foretold a coming general resurrection associated with final judgment: "All who are in the tombs will hear his voice and come out...those who have done good to the resurrection of life" (John 5:28–29). Revelation further depicts two resurrections—of the righteous and the wicked—with consequent reward or condemnation (Revelation 20:4–6). The first resurrection grants eternal life; the second brings judgment and eternal separation. These eschatological truths rest on the pattern set by Christ's rising: believers follow Him into life; unbelievers face accountability. Resurrection theology thus undergirds both the comfort of eternal life and the solemn warning of judgment. Ethical urgency and evangelistic zeal emerge from this dual horizon: proclaiming the gospel to rescue souls from judgment and to secure eternal life. Resurrection anchors hope for reunion with loved ones and motivates godly living in anticipation of the age to come.

5.5 Implications for Church and Mission

Resurrection doctrine profoundly shapes the shape and purpose of the church. Worship, sacraments, evangelism, and community life all derive their meaning from Easter morning. As the Spirit-filled community proclaims "Christ is risen," it embodies resurrection power in its gatherings and outreach. This section explores how the church's worship practices, evangelistic witness, and communal compassion reflect resurrection reality.

5.5.1 Corporate Worship and Sacraments (1 Corinthians 11:23–26)

Paul reminds the Corinthian church that the Lord's Supper proclaims Jesus' death "until he comes" (1 Corinthians 11:26), linking Eucharistic celebration directly to resurrection expectation. Likewise, baptism symbolizes burial with Christ and rising to new life (Romans 6:3–4). These sacraments enact the death–resurrection pattern, inviting participants to embody the paschal mystery. Liturgy, with its readings of resurrection narratives, paschal candles, and Easter hymns, roots corporate worship in the empty tomb. The communal re-enactment of resurrection fosters corporate identity as the Body of Christ, called to reflect His life and light. By centering gatherings on Easter themes—victory over death, new creation—the church maintains its primary focus. Sacraments thus become means of grace, applying resurrection power individually and collectively.

5.5.2 Witness and Evangelism (Acts 4:33; 1 Peter 3:15)

The early church's bold proclamation—"great grace was upon them all" (Acts 4:33)—stems from resurrection conviction. Apostolic preaching consistently centered on Christ's death and resurrection as the gospel's core (1 Corinthians 15:1–4). Peter exhorts believers to "always be prepared to make a defense to anyone who asks you for a reason for the hope that is in you" (1 Peter 3:15), urging the church to link its speech to the living reality of the risen Lord. Resurrection witness transcends cultural barriers, empowered by Spirit-given boldness (Acts 2:4). Mission strategies that continually articulate Easter heart—death has been defeated—resonate with seekers who yearn for hope. Resurrection thus remains the non-negotiable centerpiece of evangelism, motivating believers to share the good news that death is not the end but the gateway to eternal life.

5.5.3 Community of Hope and Compassion (Galatians 6:2; James 5:7–8)

A resurrection-shaped community bears one another's burdens (Galatians 6:2) and exercises patient endurance like farmers waiting for the "precious fruit of the earth" (James 5:7). Hope-filled compassion ministries—caring for orphans, widows, the poor—flow from the conviction that suffering is temporary and glory is imminent. Resurrection ethics impel solidarity with the marginalized, reflecting Christ's own compassion in earthly ministry and post-resurrection instructions (e.g., "feed my sheep," John 21:17). The church thus becomes a foretaste of new creation, embodying resurrection virtues in mutual care. This communal hope sustains perseverance amid trials and invites the world to witness an alternative society where self-giving love prevails. Resurrection life, therefore, not only transforms individual souls but reshapes corporate life toward compassion and justice.

5.6 Cultural and Ethical Renewal

Finally, resurrection theology extends its reach into every sphere of society, calling Christians to be agents of cultural renewal. Resurrection's affirmation of bodily dignity, cosmic redemption, and eschatological hope provides ethical guidelines for social, economic, and environmental engagement. As followers of the risen Christ, believers are called to manifest firstfruits of new creation in work, art, stewardship, and justice. This section examines how resurrection informs public witness and counters cultural despair.

5.6.1 Shaping Society by Resurrection Values

The doctrine of bodily resurrection affirms human dignity, mandating respect for life in all its stages—rejecting dehumanizing ideologies such as abortion, euthanasia, and human trafficking. Believers, acknowledging that every person bears God's image and is destined for resurrection, advocate policies that promote life, health, and flourishing. Resurrection values prioritize reconciliation over retaliation, mercy over cruelty, and restoration over rejection. In civic discourse, Christians can offer a vision of society where hope prevails over cynicism and compassion over indifference. By embodying resurrection virtues—grace, forgiveness, generosity—Christians act as leaven within culture, modeling an alternative ethic rooted in the empty tomb. This holistic engagement demonstrates that resurrection life transforms not only souls but societal structures.

5.6.2 Economic and Environmental Stewardship

Resurrection theology carries economic implications: just as Christ's rising transformed scarcity into abundance, believers are called to practice jubilee-inspired generosity and equitable resource distribution (Luke 4:18–19; Leviticus 25). Stewardship of creation flows from the belief that the entire world awaits liberation from corruption (Romans 8:19–22). Economic policies and business practices informed by resurrection ethics resist exploitation and environmental degradation, seeking sustainability as an expression of new creation priorities. Initiatives such as microfinance, fair-trade, and community-supported agriculture reflect the church's commitment to honoring both human dignity and creation's integrity. By integrating spiritual hope with practical stewardship, Christians pioneer holistic renewal that anticipates the world's restoration.

5.6.3 Countercultural Witness and Resistance

In a culture enamored with power and violence, resurrection witness subverts normative paradigms by embracing nonviolence and forgiveness—exemplified in Jesus' injunction "turn the other cheek" (Matthew 5:39). Radical hospitality toward strangers and enemies embodies the open-tomb ethos that overcomes fear with welcome. Resurrection identity resists oppressive systems, advocating for the voiceless and marginalized in solidarity with Christ's suffering body. Artistic expressions—literature, film, music—infused with resurrection themes challenge societal despair by depicting hope's triumph over despair. Through such countercultural engagement, the church testifies that resurrection life offers a credible alternative to the world's cycles of violence and dehumanization. This resistance anticipates the final renewal when God will make "all things new" (Revelation 21:5).

Conclusion The resurrection of Jesus stands as the cornerstone upon which the entire Christian edifice is built. It is the wellspring of personal victory over sin and death, supplying assurance that our justification and adoption are irrevocable. Resurrection life empowers sanctification, infusing ethical living with divine vitality. It inaugurates the kingdom of God, guarantees bodily renewal, and frames our eschatological hope amid final judgment. For the church, resurrection shapes worship, fuels evangelism, and cultivates communities of compassion. Beyond ecclesial boundaries, resurrection theology offers society a vision of transformed humanity and restored creation. As Christians continue to bear witness to the risen Lord, they participate in a narrative that transcends every cultural context and speaks to the deepest longings of the human heart. May this theological foundation not only inform the mind but ignite spiritual vitality, driving the church to live as resurrection people in a world desperate for new life.

Chapter 6: The Resurrection and the Church

The resurrection of Jesus Christ not only validates His victory over sin and death but also serves as the foundational event that shapes the identity, worship, mission, ethics, unity, and eschatological hope of the Christian community. Far from being an isolated miracle, Easter morning inaugurates a new reality in which the risen Lord indwells His people, empowers them for witness, and calls them into transformation. In this chapter, we will explore how the resurrection gives birth to the "Body of Christ," defines corporate worship as a living memorial, fuels global mission, reshapes communal ethics, breaks down barriers between diverse believers, and anchors the church's forward-looking hope. Drawing on key New Testament texts—from Pauline epistles to Acts and Revelation—we will see that the risen Christ remains the active center of ecclesial life. As we unpack these themes, we will discover that every facet of the church's existence flows from the empty tomb, calling each generation to live as resurrection people in a world that still groans for renewal.

6.1 The Body of Christ: Identity and Unity

6.1.1 Baptism into Resurrection Life

Paul's teaching in Romans 6:3–5 affirms that baptism into Christ's death leads believers to walk in newness of life through His resurrection. In this sacrament, the church publicly identifies with Jesus' burial—going down into the waters—and with His rising—emerging to new life (Colossians 2:12). Baptism thus marks the initiation into the one Body of Christ, transcending ethnic, social, and gender divides (1 Corinthians 12:13). It cements the reality that every believer shares organically in Christ's death to sin and resurrection to righteousness. This union forms the basis for Christian identity—"no longer I who live, but Christ lives in me" (Galatians 2:20). The ongoing significance of baptism lies not only in the initial rite but in its daily implications: believers live out their baptismal calling through continual dying to self and rising to the Spirit (Romans 6:6–11). By rooting ecclesial belonging in resurrection, baptism grounds the church's identity in divine action rather than human achievement.

6.1.2 Spiritual Gifts and Ministries

Ephesians 4:11–16 and 1 Corinthians 12:4–11 reveal that the risen Christ dispenses diverse spiritual gifts—apostles, prophets, evangelists, pastors, teachers—by the Holy Spirit for the building up of His Body. These ministries flow from resurrection authority: "He gave gifts to men" (Ephesians 4:8). No gift stands apart; each operates within the interdependent unity of the church, contributing to maturity in faith and service. Healing and miracles, also Christ-wrought, testify to the ongoing presence of resurrection power (Acts 3:6–8). By integrating gifts into mutual edification, the church reflects its unity amid diversity, fulfilling Paul's prayer that we attain "to the measure of the stature of the fullness of Christ" (Ephesians 4:13). Resurrection life energizes every ministry, ensuring that no calling is mundane and no role insignificant. When the Body functions with sacrificial love and humility (1 Corinthians 13), it embodies the risen Lord's intention for a healthy, vibrant community.

6.1.3 Unity in Diversity: One Body, Many Parts

Paul's extended metaphor in 1 Corinthians 12:12–27 stresses that the church, like a human body, comprises many members with distinct functions yet forms one organism. Each part—eye, hand, foot—matters, and no member can claim independence or superiority. Resurrection reality knits this diversity together: we "have been baptized into one body" (v. 13). When one member suffers, all suffer; when one member is honored, all rejoice (v. 26). This interdependence safeguards against fragmentation and promotes genuine care. In practical terms, congregations demonstrate this unity by sharing resources, offering mutual support, and celebrating each other's gifts. The risen Lord, through His Spirit, binds believers across cultural and theological differences, calling them into a shared mission. Resurrection unity thus becomes a powerful witness to the world of God's reconciling work in Christ.

6.1.4 The Church as Bride and Body of Christ

Paul and the author of Revelation employ bridal imagery to describe the church's relationship to Christ. In Ephesians 5:25–27, husbands are told to love their wives "as Christ loved the church and gave himself up for her," cleansing her to present her "holy and without blemish." Revelation 19:7–9 envisions the marriage supper of the Lamb, where the church, clothed in "fine linen, bright and pure," celebrates union with her Bridegroom. The resurrection serves as the seal of Christ's faithfulness to His bride—He died and rose again, demonstrating love that overcomes death. This imagery shapes corporate worship and personal devotion, inspiring purity, commitment, and anticipation of final consummation. As the Body, the church lives out this bridal identity in communal life—nurturing intimate fellowship with Christ and reflecting His love to a watching world.

6.2 Worship as Resurrection Memorial

6.2.1 Eucharist: Proclaiming Death and Resurrection

In 1 Corinthians 11:23–26, Paul records Jesus' words at the Last Supper: "This is my body… Do this in remembrance of me… for as often as you eat this bread and drink the cup, you proclaim the Lord's death until he comes." The Eucharist transcends mere remembrance to become a living proclamation of Christ's death and resurrection. The elements of bread and wine embody the broken body and shed blood of the risen Lord, drawing participants into the Paschal mystery. Every celebration of the Lord's Supper connects believers across time and space to the original Easter event, anchoring corporate worship in resurrection truth. Through Eucharistic participation, the church experiences the risen Christ's presence and receives strength for sanctified living and mission. Eucharist thus functions as both sacrament—means of grace—and summons to embody resurrection life in the world.

6.2.2 Baptism: Participation in Christ's Death and Rising

Baptism, second only to Eucharist in liturgical prominence, reiterates union with Christ's death and resurrection (Romans 6:4; Colossians 2:12). As new disciples are immersed and raised from the water, the congregation witnesses the outward sign of inner transformation—dying to sin's dominion and rising to new life. In liturgical contexts, baptismal vows proclaim the centrality of resurrection faith: turning from darkness to light, renouncing evil, and affirming Christ's lordship. The church, as a baptized community, commits itself to nurture the newly baptized through catechesis, fellowship, and ongoing discipleship. By celebrating baptism regularly—both infant and believer's baptism—churches reinforce identity in the risen Lord and affirm the ongoing work of new creation among believers.

6.2.3 The Easter Vigil and Paschal Liturgy

The Easter Vigil—a liturgy celebrated on Holy Saturday night—immerses the church in the ebb and flow of salvation history. Beginning in darkness, the congregation lights the new Paschal candle, symbolizing Christ, the Light of the world (John 8:12), rising from the tomb. Scripture readings trace God's redemptive acts from Creation through the Prophets, culminating in the proclamation of resurrection. Water and oil ceremonies incorporate baptismal and confirmation rites, echoing new Covenant promises (Jeremiah 31:31–34). The vigil reaches its crescendo with the first Easter Eucharist, celebrating the risen Lord's presence. This liturgy integrates Word and sacrament, memory and mission, casting worshipers into a rhythm that continually points back to Easter and forward to final consummation. The Paschal liturgy thus sanctifies time itself, declaring that every Christian life flows from the empty tomb.

6.2.4 Resurrection Hymns and the Theology of Praise

From earliest patristic texts to modern hymnals, the church's songbook brims with resurrection themes. Hymns like "Christ the Lord Is Risen Today," "Jesus Christ Is Risen Today," and the ancient Exsultet weave together theological affirmation and joyous praise. Musical and poetic expressions become vehicles for confessing Easter reality with both mind and heart. Visual arts—icons, paintings, stained glass—portray the empty tomb, the three Marys, and Christ's triumphant ascent, reinforcing liturgical proclamation. By engaging body, voice, and imagination, hymnody and art shape a worship ethos steeped in resurrection joy. This culture of praise sustains believers in trials and summons them to proclaim hope to a world in darkness. In praising the risen Lord, the church embodies the glad news that death has been conquered.

6.3 Mission and Witness: From Jerusalem to the Ends of the Earth

6.3.1 The Great Commission and Resurrection Authority

Matthew 28:18–20 links resurrection vindication directly to global mission: "All authority... has been given to me." With sovereign authority over heaven and earth, the risen Christ commands disciples to "go and make disciples of all nations... teaching them to observe all that I have commanded you." The trinitarian baptismal formula underscores the cosmic scope of this mandate. By commissioning both Jews and Gentiles, Jesus extends resurrection hope to every people group. The promise "I am with you always" (v. 20) assures continuous presence and empowerment. Resurrection thus undergirds missionary urgency and theological foundation, driving the church to cross cultural boundaries with the gospel.

6.3.2 Empowerment by the Spirit: Resurrection and Pentecost

Acts 1:8 foreshadows Pentecost: "You will receive power when the Holy Spirit has come upon you, and you will be my witnesses... to the end of the earth." The Spirit's descent on the day of Pentecost (Acts 2) fulfills Jesus' resurrection promise, equipping the church for bold proclamation and miraculous signs. This empowerment reflects the same power that raised Christ (Ephesians 1:19–20), now at work in the community. The Spirit unifies diverse tongues and cultures, mirroring resurrection unity in the Body. Mission thereafter flows from Spirit-filled witness, confirming the risen Lord's presence and compelling gospel advance. Resurrection and Pentecost together inaugurate the church's global vocation.

6.3.3 Signs, Wonders, and Bold Proclamation

The book of Acts records that the apostles accompanied bold preaching of the resurrection with signs and wonders: healings (Acts 3:6–8), exorcisms (Acts 16:18), and miraculous rescues (Acts 5:16). These demonstrations verified Christ's living presence and authenticated the apostolic message.

Peter's prayer for boldness (Acts 4:29–31) yielded a fresh outpouring of the Spirit, emboldening the church amid persecution. Such acts served not as ends in themselves but as catalysts for faith—drawing crowds to the message of Christ's victory. Resurrection power in mission challenges spiritual indifference and testifies that true hope overcomes death. Contemporary witnesses therefore embrace both proclamation and compassionate power ministry, reflecting the holistic gospel of life in Christ.

6.3.4 Missional Communities Modeled on Emmaus and the Upper Room

Luke's resurrection accounts in Luke 24:13–35 (Emmaus) and Luke 24:36–43 (Upper Room) present models for small-group discipleship and mission. On the road to Emmaus, the combination of Scripture exposition and breaking of bread opened disciples' eyes to the risen Lord. In the locked room, Jesus offered peace, showed His wounds, and shared a meal to confirm His physical resurrection. These prototypes inform contemporary missional communities: gatherings that integrate Word, table, and mutual support. Such communities spawn personal transformation and mission sending— members, like the Emmaus disciples, "returned at once" to proclaim the news (Luke 24:33). The Upper Room pattern— peace greeting, communal fellowship, commissioning— calibrates church life for both worship and outreach. Resurrection-shaped small groups thus become laboratories for living and proclaiming Easter truth.

6.4 Ethics and Community: Resurrection-Shaped Living

6.4.1 Koinōnia: Fellowship in Resurrection Life

Acts 2:42–47 depicts the early church devoted to "the apostles' teaching and fellowship [koinōnia], to the breaking of bread and the prayers." Their lives were characterized by shared possessions and meeting each other's needs, reflecting the common life birthed by resurrection. Koinōnia signifies deep mutual participation in Christ's life and in one another's joys and sufferings (1 Corinthians 12:26). Resurrection power motivates radical generosity and authentic community, where barriers of fear and self-interest dissolve. This fellowship was not utopian fantasy but Spirit-enabled reality that drew others to Christ. Contemporary churches rooted in koinōnia prioritize small-group life, shared meal times, and stewardship, displaying resurrection hospitality. Such communities embody the new creation, offering a foretaste of perfected fellowship.

6.4.2 Mutual Edification and Church Discipline

Paul addresses corrective care in 1 Corinthians 5 and Galatians 6:1–2, instructing believers to restore erring members gently and to bear one another's burdens. Resurrection hope shapes this discipline: it seeks restoration, not exclusion, based on the assurance that God transforms hearts. The goal of church discipline is both honor for Christ and healing within the Body, reflecting the reconciling work of the risen Lord. Mutual edification arises when members encourage one another to exercise their gifts and pursue holiness (Ephesians 4:29). Resurrection ethics support accountability structures that blend truth and grace, ensuring that correction flows from love for the Body. In this way, the community becomes a secure environment for growth, reflecting Christ's restorative power.

6.4.3 Social Justice and Compassion as Resurrection Fruit

James insists that "faith without works is dead" (James 2:17), and Proverbs urges believers to "open your mouth for the mute…defend the rights of the poor and needy" (Prov. 31:8–9). Resurrection life propels the church into ministries of justice and compassion—from feeding the hungry to advocating for the oppressed. Christ's rising from the margins of human contempt to cosmic lordship compels solidarity with those whom society discards. Resurrection ethics resist exploitation and champion dignity, echoing Jesus' concern for the least of these (Matthew 25:40). Compassion ministries—hospices, orphan care, anti-trafficking—demonstrate that

Easter hope transforms social structures and individual lives. Thus, the church's service to society becomes a visible sign of resurrection's renewing power.

6.4.4 Resurrection Hope in Hospitality and Care

Peter exhorts believers to "show hospitality to one another without grumbling" (1 Peter 4:9) and to use their gifts "to serve one another" (v. 10). Hospitality—a central practice in biblical culture—embodies resurrection's reversal of fear and alienation. Welcoming strangers, providing shelter, and sharing table fellowship incarnate Christ's open tomb. Early Christians risked social stigma to care for the sick and marginalized, portraying resurrection compassion in concrete acts. In contemporary contexts, intentional hospitality ministries—home fellowships, refugee resettlement, community meals—continue this legacy. By embodying resurrection care, the church displays the reconciling and nourishing love of the risen Lord to a fragmented world.

6.5 Unity, Diversity, and Ecumenical Implications

6.5.1 One Body in Christ, Breaking Walls of Hostility

Ephesians 2:14–16 proclaims that Christ, our peace, has "broken down... the dividing wall of hostility" between Jew and Gentile, creating one new humanity. Resurrection life breaches every barrier—ethnic, cultural, socioeconomic—that divides human beings. The empty tomb dismantles prejudices and fosters reconciliation within the Body of Christ. In practice, churches pursue integrated worship, joint mission partnerships, and interracial leadership teams to embody this unity. By celebrating diverse gifts and backgrounds under resurrection lordship, the church models the reconciled kingdom that reaches beyond Sunday gatherings to societal transformation.

6.5.2 Reconciling Jew and Gentile in Resurrection Hope

Galatians 3:28 affirms that "in Christ Jesus… there is neither Jew nor Greek." Resurrection erases the distinction rooted in the Law, uniting believers into Abraham's seed (Galatians 3:29). Acts chronicles the church's grappling with Gentile inclusion—Peter's vision (Acts 10), the Jerusalem Council (Acts 15)—showing that resurrection compelled the church to expand its covenantal boundaries. Today, dialogues between Jewish and Gentile believers, Messianic congregations, and interdenominational movements honor this legacy. Resurrection hope thus sustains reconciliation across millennia, reminding the church that its unity precedes and transcends cultural and historical divides.

6.5.3 Cultivating Interchurch Unity and Cooperation

Historic creeds—the Nicene, Apostles', Chalcedonian—centrally confess Christ's death and resurrection, providing common theological ground for diverse traditions. Shared liturgical practices—Easter Vigil, Paschal Liturgy—further unite Christians across denominational lines. Joint mission initiatives, ecumenical councils, and cooperative relief efforts demonstrate resurrection unity in action. While recognizing doctrinal differences, Christians commit to collaboration where core confessions align on the risen Christ. This cooperative spirit amplifies witness and honors the risen Lord's prayer "that they may all be one" (John 17:21).

6.5.4 Global Church Fellowship and the Kingdom of God

The communion of saints, spanning continents and centuries, celebrates the resurrection as the church's unifying center. Every culture's expression—African praise songs, Asian calligraphy icons, Latin American processions—proclaims "Christ is risen"! Together, these myriad voices anticipate the wedding feast of the Lamb (Revelation 19:9), affirming that the church is a foretaste of the global, eternal assembly. Resurrection thus shapes a fellowship that transcends geography, social strata, and time, reflecting the universality of Christ's reign.

6.6 Eschatological Dimension of the Church

6.6.1 The Church as Firstfruits Community

James 1:18 and Revelation 14:4 present the church as God's firstfruits—a consecrated harvest offering to inaugurate the new creation. Resurrection places believers at the vanguard of cosmic renewal, entrusted to bear witness to coming restoration. As firstfruits, the church enjoys anticipatory tastes of resurrection life—cultivating peace, justice, and holiness. This status inspires sacrificial living and hopeful expectation, motivating the community to embody kingdom values ahead of full consummation.

6.6.2 Living Between the "Already" and "Not Yet"

Paul's theology of the resurrection—Christ the firstfruits, then those who belong to Him (1 Corinthians 15:20–23)—frames the "already/not yet" tension. The church exists in the overlap of ages: resurrected life dwells within but awaits full manifestation. This tension shapes discipleship, calling believers to live holy lives amid an unredeemed world. Hope becomes the engine for mission and ethics, driving perseverance and steadfastness until Christ's return.

6.6.3 Participation in Final Resurrection and Judgment

Jesus taught of a general resurrection "to life" and "to judgment" (John 5:28–29). Revelation 20:4–6 describes the blessedness of the first resurrection—they "will be priests of God and of Christ" and "reign with him a thousand years." The church's vocation includes warning of judgment and proclaiming grace to all who will come. Resurrection conviction undergirds evangelism and ethical urgency, as every life stands before the risen Judge. The church prepares people for both destiny and accountability.

6.6.4 Hope of New Heavens and New Earth

Revelation 21:1–4 unveils God's promise of a new heaven and new earth, where death and mourning are no more. The church, empowered by resurrection, serves as a sign and agent of this future reality, stewarding creation and ministering healing in anticipation of cosmic renewal. This eschatological hope liberates Christians from worldly attachments and fuels commitment to justice, mercy, and care for creation. As participants in the unfolding drama of redemption, believers live with eyes fixed on the final consummation where the risen Christ dwells forever with His people.

Conclusion From the moment Mary Magdalene ran with news of the empty tomb to the global mission empowered by Pentecost, the resurrection has irrevocably shaped the church's identity, worship, mission, ethics, unity, and hope. Baptism and Eucharist enshrine Christ's death and rising in the rhythms of communal life, while diverse ministries manifest resurrection power in service. Ethical imperatives flow from new-creation life, driving justice, compassion, and hospitality. Resurrection shatters every barrier—Jew and Gentile, rich and poor, male and female—uniting believers into one Body and Bride of the risen Lord. As the firstfruits of a cosmic harvest, the church lives in the tension of "already" and "not yet," proclaiming both judgment and grace as it anticipates Christ's return. Ultimately, the resurrection anchors the church's eschatological vision of a new heaven and new earth, where death is no more and joy is everlasting. May this chapter's reflections equip the church to embody resurrection reality in every context, as the world awaits the full unveiling of God's redemptive purposes.

Chapter 7: Living Resurrection—Everyday Implications

The reality of Christ's resurrection extends far beyond a once-for-all miracle celebrated on Easter morning; it reshapes every dimension of the Christian's daily existence. When Jesus broke the bonds of death, He inaugurated a new way of life—one marked by freedom from sin, hope amid suffering, and power for service. This resurrection life infuses ordinary routines with divine significance, transforming prayer, work, relationships, and even rest into opportunities to witness the risen Lord. In this chapter, we explore how believers can live out Easter's victory in the rhythms of each day. From spiritual formation practices that keep Easter dawn at the forefront of our minds, to vocation understood as resurrection ministry, to community life steeped in compassion and justice, every aspect of our existence finds its North Star in the empty tomb. As we delve into these everyday implications, may we discover how the same power that raised Christ from the dead empowers us to bear fruit for God's kingdom now and to anticipate the new creation yet to come.

7.1 Spiritual Formation in Resurrection Power

7.1.1 Daily Remembrance and Renewal

The dawn of each new day offers a natural opportunity to recall Christ's rising and to renew our minds in resurrection truth. Morning prayer that begins with the exclamation "Christ is risen!" intentionally grounds our thoughts in Easter's triumph before the world's demands crowd in. Psalm 5:3 models this posture: "O LORD, in the morning you hear my voice; in the morning I prepare a sacrifice for you and watch." By combining the ancient pattern of daily sacrifice with contemporary prayers of gratitude for new mercies (Lamentations 3:22–23), believers stitch resurrection hope into the fabric of ordinary routines. Even brief prayer rhythms—such as the "Easter doxology," "Thanks be to God who gives us the victory through our Lord Jesus Christ" (1 Corinthians 15:57)—can become internalized, surfacing spontaneously when faced with challenges. Journaling a one-sentence thanksgiving each dawn cultivates a habit of remembrance that shapes attitudes throughout the day. Over time, this practice fosters resilience: when trials arrive, the mind instinctively turns to the risen Lord rather than to despair. Thus, daily rituals of remembrance keep the power of Easter alive in the heart's earliest moments.

7.1.2 Scripture as Encounter with the Risen Lord

Reading the Gospels and Paul's resurrection chapters becomes more than an academic exercise when approached contemplatively. Lectio divina invites a slow, prayerful interaction with passages such as Luke 24:13–35, where the Emmaus disciples' hearts "burned within" as Jesus opened the Scriptures, and 1 Corinthians 15, where Paul expounds the meaning of resurrection. By meditating on these texts over several days, readers transition from mere information to intimate encounter. Reflective questions—"Lord, where do I still cling to death rather than embrace new life?" or "What part of my life needs the light of Your resurrection?"—guide the Spirit's illumination. Journaling insights and prayers sparked by these readings produces a living record of spiritual growth. Over time, Scripture reading transforms from duty to delight, as the risen Christ reveals Himself in every line. This dynamic approach integrates biblical formation with the ongoing reality of resurrection, ensuring that the Word continually shapes life.

7.1.3 Prayer Empowered by Resurrection Hope

Prayer in the name of Jesus (John 14:13–14) carries the authority of Easter: because Christ reigns, His followers can approach the Father with confidence. This resolve reshapes intercession, transforming it from timid requests into expectant petitions. When believers pray for healing, reconciliation, or breakthrough, they do so with the resurrection as their foundation—death's power has been broken, and hope endures (Romans 15:13). Praying through baptisms—memorials of death and resurrection—intensifies this confidence, as each request rides on the wave of Christ's victory. When ministering to those in dark "tombs" of depression or addiction, intercessors stand on the promise that Jesus commands "you will know the truth, and the truth will set you free" (John 8:32). Prayers shaped by resurrection hope become catalysts for transformation, not only for individuals but for communities. In this way, the church prays not from human limitation but from the vantage point of risen life.

7.1.4 Worship Beyond the Sunday Gathering

While Sunday worship remains the cornerstone of corporate celebration, small "mini-Easters" throughout the week nurture continual awareness of resurrection. Families or house churches gathering midweek to read a resurrection narrative, light a candle, and share testimonies of God's work in their lives keep Easter central. Spontaneous songs of praise—bursting forth when God provides a breakthrough, when reconciliation occurs, or when justice prevails—become the echo of that first Easter dawn. Displaying a simple art piece or icon of the empty tomb in a living room can serve as a visual liturgy, reminding all who enter that Christ's victory stands at the heart of home life. These practices reinforce the truth that worship is not confined to a sanctuary but flows from every context where resurrection reality is proclaimed by deed and word. Such continuous worship nurtures a posture of adoration and gratitude that anchors daily life in the risen Lord.

7.2 Vocation and Work as Resurrection Ministry

7.2.1 Work as Worship in the New Creation

Colossians 3:23 exhorts believers to "work heartily, as for the Lord and not for men," framing daily labor as participation in God's renewal of all things. Understanding work as "worship in disguise" transforms mundane tasks—emails, presentations, caregiving—into offerings before the throne, reflecting the new creation dynamics inaugurated by Easter. When teachers shape minds, they become co-laborers in the Spirit's transformative work. When healthcare workers serve patients with compassion, they embody Christ's resurrecting power over sickness. The risen Lord's own early post-resurrection acts—preparing breakfast for His disciples by the Sea of Galilee (John 21:9)—model the dignity of daily labor. By integrating excellence, creativity, and joy into our vocations, we bear witness to the God who makes all things new (Revelation 21:5). This holistic vision counters the sacred–secular divide, ensuring that every workplace becomes a stage for resurrection life to shine.

7.2.2 Integrity, Justice, and Economic Stewardship

Resurrection life repudiates exploitative economic practices by upholding fairness and stewardship. Proverbs 16:11 declares, "A just balance and scales are the LORD's; all the weights in the bag are his work." Businesses that pay fair wages, maintain honest books, and steward resources sustainably demonstrate the risen Lord's concern for the marginalized. Jubilee rhythms (Leviticus 25) echo Easter principles—periodic rest for land and debt forgiveness—offering a blueprint for contemporary economic renewal. Churches can promote cooperative enterprises, microfinance for small entrepreneurs, and ethical consumption as tangible expressions of resurrection hope. By conducting commerce in ways that uplift human dignity and care for creation, Christians reflect the economic dimension of God's new creation. Resurrection ministry in the marketplace thus transforms proprietary gain into kingdom investment, leveraging wealth for holistic flourishing.

7.2.3 Vocation Discerning under Resurrection Light

Discerning one's calling in light of Easter involves aligning personal gifts with kingdom needs. Ephesians 2:10 reminds believers they are "created in Christ Jesus for good works, which God prepared beforehand." As individuals prayerfully explore their abilities and passions, they seek where the risen Lord invites them to serve. Career transitions become kairos moments: stepping from a high-paying role into nonprofit work, shifting from self-focused ambition to community-centered service. Balancing ambition with a servant's heart (Philippians 2:5–8) prevents vocational success from overshadowing spiritual formation. Community discernment—mentoring, pastoral guidance, peer accountability—helps individuals test callings against resurrection values. When vocation is understood not primarily as personal advancement but as participation in God's redemptive work, every occupational path becomes a sphere for resurrection ministry.

7.3 Relationships and Community Life

7.3.1 Family as Domestic Resurrection Community

The home provides the first context for living out Easter's implications. Household devotions centered on resurrection narratives—reading Luke 24, singing an Easter hymn at supper—instill hope in children and spouses alike. Parenting becomes an exercise in nurturing "little resurrection people," guiding youngsters toward living faith through Deuteronomy 6:6–7 style practices: teaching on the way, talking at home and on the road. Marital love, grounded in mutual sacrifice, mirrors Christ's giving of Himself for the church (Ephesians 5:25). When parents and children practice forgiveness, hospitality, and service within the home, they embody healed relationships that point beyond mere coexistence to the new creation family. Family rhythms—shared meals, rest, celebration—become sacramental spaces where resurrection life is lived out concretely. In these domestic settings, the first seeds of communal transformation are sown.

7.3.2 Friendship, Accountability, and Mutual Care

Deep friendships offer channels for resurrection community to flourish. James 5:16 urges believers to "confess your sins to one another and pray for one another, that you may be healed." Small discipleship groups incorporate confession, encouragement, and prayer into regular meetings, reflecting the mutual solidarity birthed by Easter. Sharing burdens— whether financial struggles, health crises, or relational conflicts—in light of Galatians 6:2 ("Bear one another's burdens, and so fulfill the law of Christ") creates resilience within the church. Authentic accountability partners walk together through temptations, reminding each other of resurrection identity when doubt creeps in. Such friendships become living reminders that the risen Lord journeys with us through valleys and mountaintops alike, forging bonds of trust that testify to Christ's reconciling power.

7.3.3 Hospitality at the Open Table

Hospitality emerges as a hallmark of resurrection-shaped community. Inviting neighbors, unbelieving friends, and even strangers to Easter-shaped meals offers tangible glimpses of God's banquet table (1 Peter 4:9). Celebrating diversity around the table—feasting on foods from various cultures— prefigures the marriage supper of the Lamb, where "people from every tribe and language and people and nation" assemble (Revelation 19:9). Home-based Eucharistic reflections, where believers share bread and cup in the domestic sphere, blur the line between table fellowship and public worship, reminding guests that resurrection joy overflows private devotion. These gatherings become microcosms of the church's global family, proclaiming by word and deed that in Christ, barriers fall and all are welcome. Through such hospitality, the open tomb translates into open arms and open tables.

7.4 Witness in Suffering and Service

7.4.1 Empathy Born of Christ's Passion and Triumph

Christ's journey through suffering to resurrection equips believers to enter into others' pain with genuine empathy. Hebrews 4:15 assures us that Jesus "has been tempted in every way, just as we are—yet without sin," making Him a sympathetic high priest. When Christians minister to those in grief, addiction, or chronic illness, they do so not merely as well-meaning volunteers but as fellow sufferers who know both the shadow of death and the light of resurrection. Mourning with those who mourn (Romans 12:15) becomes a sacred act, pointing the afflicted toward the hope that outlasts every hardship. Personal testimonies of how resurrection sustained one through adversity become powerful tools for pastoral care. In these encounters, Easter transforms compassion from theory into lived solidarity.

7.4.2 Justice, Advocacy, and Spiritual Warfare

Resurrection life fuels the church's engagement in spiritual and social battles. Jesus' proclamation in Luke 4:18–19—"He has sent me…to proclaim liberty to the captives"—remains the banner of justice ministries that confront systemic evil. Prayer teams intercede against human trafficking, racism, and other forms of oppression, confident that "greater is he who is in you than he who is in the world" (1 John 4:4). Advocacy for immigrants, the incarcerated, and the marginalized draws on resurrection ethics that honor human dignity. Spiritual warfare, when practiced biblically, involves binding demonic principalities and loosing gospel freedom (Matthew 18:18), confident that Christ's resurrection shattered evil's power. By coupling advocacy with prayer, the church enacts a holistic witness to the implications of Easter victory.

7.4.3 Peacemaking and Forgiveness as Resurrection Witness

Jesus' command to forgive seventy-seven times (Matthew 18:22) and to love enemies (Matthew 5:44) springs directly from His triumph over death. Forgiveness, while counterintuitive, manifests resurrection power by breaking cycles of retaliation and bitterness. Peacemakers—those who actively seek reconciliation—are called "children of God" (Matthew 5:9), reflecting the reconciling work of the risen Christ. Churches can offer reconciliation ministries that train couples, families, and communities in biblical peacemaking. When forgiven people extend grace to their offenders, they embody Easter's reversal: out of death comes new life, out of guilt comes liberating pardon. This countercultural practice showcases that resurrection transforms hearts and societies alike.

7.5 Physical Health, Sabbath Rest, and Creation Care

7.5.1 Body as Temple of the Risen Lord

Paul reminds Corinthian believers that their bodies are "temples of the Holy Spirit" (1 Corinthians 6:19–20), indwelled by the risen Christ. Physical health, then, is not a self-indulgent pursuit but an act of stewardship that honors God's investment in our bodies. Regular exercise, balanced nutrition, and adequate sleep reflect gratitude for the gift of resurrection life. Healthcare ministries—in churches, clinics, or nursing care—participate in Jesus' healing ministry, extending resurrection's wholeness to the sick and vulnerable. Celebrating the body's dignity also involves advocating for those with disabilities, ensuring that all persons are included and honored as bearers of divine image. In caring for bodies, the church testifies to the future promise of glorified, imperishable bodies raised with Christ (1 Corinthians 15:42–44).

7.5.2 Sabbath Rhythms of Rest and Renewal

God instituted the Sabbath on the seventh day, setting a pattern of rest after creative work (Exodus 20:8–11). Resurrection life reframes Sabbath rest as both a gift and an act of trust in God's ongoing provision. Modern practices—digital sabbaths, unplugged weekends, or day-long retreats—

offer respite from frenetic pace, allowing believers to reconnect with Creator. Such rhythms counter burnout and foster mental health, aligning with Jesus' invitation in Matthew 11:28–29 to find rest in Him. Extended sabbath seasons—retreats, pilgrimages, and extended breaks—provide deeper reorientation in resurrection presence. By honoring Sabbath, the church embodies the firstfruits of new creation, living in the confidence that God's rest awaits His people in eternity.

7.5.3 Environmental Stewardship and New Creation Care

Romans 8:19–22 reveals that creation itself groans for liberation from decay, anticipating the children of God's adoption in resurrection glory. Environmental stewardship thus flows from Easter hope—caring for land, water, and air as sacred charges. Church initiatives—community gardens, recycling programs, conservation advocacy—participate in creation's redemption. Theological reflection on new creation (Revelation 21:1–5) casts ecology as worship, inviting believers to cultivate beauty and biodiversity. By reducing waste, supporting renewable energy, and championing environmental justice, Christians demonstrate that resurrection life renews both humanity and the earth. Such integrative care aligns practical action with the cosmic scope of Christ's triumph over decay.

7.6 Cultural Engagement and Creativity

7.6.1 Arts, Music, and Storytelling as Resurrection Proclamation

Human creativity bears the imprint of its Creator and can articulate Easter's power in fresh idioms. Visual artists capture the empty tomb, the harrowing of hell, and the ascension with colors and forms that convey hope beyond words. Musicians compose anthems and intimate hymns that narrate resurrection narratives, leading congregations into encounters with the living Lord. Filmmakers, playwrights, and novelists weave stories of redemption that echo Easter's themes of loss and new life. Churches can host arts festivals, concerts, and exhibitions that invite the wider community to experience resurrection truth. When creativity is rooted in Easter theology, it becomes a powerful witness that transcends cultural barriers. In this way, beauty itself proclaims the risen King.

7.6.2 Technology, Media, and Gospel Innovation

Digital platforms offer unprecedented channels for broadcasting resurrection testimonies. Social media stories, livestreamed services, podcasts, and blogs can share first-person accounts of resurrection hope in everyday contexts. Virtual small groups replicate the Emmaus road experience, discussing Scripture and sharing life in online spaces. Emerging technologies—virtual reality Bible experiences, interactive apps for prayer and meditation—equip believers to encounter the risen Lord in new ways. Ethical guidelines, grounded in Jesus' example of humility and service, ensure that technology serves rather than dominates church life. By innovating responsibly, the church amplifies Easter's impact in a tech-driven age, reaching the ends of the earth with the message of life.

7.7 Resilience and Hope in Trials

7.7.1 Anchoring in Resurrection amidst Anxiety and Loss

Anxiety, depression, and grief confront many in the modern world, yet resurrection offers a firm anchor for the soul. Practices such as gratitude journaling—recording daily evidences of God's faithfulness—combat despair by redirecting focus to resurrection realities. Group lament gatherings allow collective mourning that transitions to praise, mirroring the shift from Good Friday sorrow to Easter joy. Pastoral counseling that integrates narrative therapy with resurrection hope helps individuals rewrite their stories against death's finality. By recalling Christ's victory over the grave, believers find courage to face medical diagnoses, financial crises, and relational ruptures. Resurrection theology thus undergirds mental health ministries, providing companions for those in darkness.

7.7.2 Community Support and Mutual Encouragement

Small-group check-ins—weekly calls or messages—sustain hope during prolonged hardship. Peer support networks within churches train "resurrection companions" who listen, pray, and share coping tools. When crises strike—a pandemic, natural disaster, personal tragedy—the church mobilizes rapid response teams offering practical aid and spiritual comfort. Testimonies of God's provision and miracles witness to resurrection power, spurring gratitude and faith in others. These mutual encouragement structures ensure that no one walks alone, reflecting Galatians 6:2's call to bear one another's burdens. In this communal embrace, resurrection hope is not abstract doctrine but lived solidarity.

7.8 Anticipating Final Fulfillment

7.8.1 Living on the "Tip-toe of Eternity"

1 Thessalonians 4:16–17 promises that Christ will return with a shout, and the dead in Christ will rise first, followed by rapture of living believers. This vivid image of sudden cosmic reversal inspires Christians to "live in the light" (Romans 13:12), maintaining moral readiness and spiritual alertness. Ethical choices—from generosity to peacemaking—are fueled by awareness that time is limited and eternity beckons. Sermons that emphasize the parousia encourage congregations to cultivate character and mission as though the trumpet might sound at any moment. This posture prevents complacency, ensuring that resurrection hope remains a dynamic force shaping priorities and actions today.

7.8.2 Evangelism as Participation in the Final Harvest

Jesus compared the world to a great harvest, urging His followers to pray, "The harvest is plentiful, but the laborers are few" (Luke 10:2). Resurrection ministry extends this metaphor: sharing Christ's victory over death invites others into the firstfruits of new creation. Every personal testimony, cross-cultural mission trip, and neighborhood outreach becomes participation in the final ingathering. Churches can train members in relational evangelism, equipping them with resurrection narratives and apologetic resources. Acts of service—feeding the hungry, caring for widows—accompany proclamation, demonstrating that resurrection life meets both spiritual and material needs. Through such holistic engagement, the church plays its part in the coming harvest, confident that the risen Lord is at work drawing souls into His kingdom.

Conclusion Living resurrection is more than occasional exuberance on Easter Sunday; it is the heartbeat of every Christian's life, infusing prayer, work, relationships, suffering, and creative expression with the power of the empty tomb. From dawn prayers that calibrate our hearts to resurrection truth, to workplace ethics that testify to Christ's reign, to communities of hospitality that prefigure the marriage supper of the Lamb, believers embody Easter's implications in diverse and dynamic ways. Resilience in trials becomes possible when the same power that raised Jesus strengthens the soul; cultural engagement and technology become platforms for proclaiming life where death once held sway. Finally, as we await Christ's return, our lives become living epistles of the final harvest, bearing witness that the grave has lost its victory. May this exploration ignite fresh imagination and deepen commitment to live each day as ambassadors of the risen King, anticipating the full renewal of heaven and earth.

Chapter 8: Resurrection Power for Ministry

The resurrection of Jesus Christ did not merely conclude His earthly ministry; it inaugurated a dynamic movement of divine power that continues to transform lives and communities. In the wake of Easter morning, the same life-giving energy that raised Jesus from the dead has been unleashed in the church, equipping ministers and laypeople alike to bear witness, heal the broken, pursue justice, and invite the world into fellowship with the living Lord. This chapter explores how resurrection power shapes every aspect of Christian ministry—forming our identity, empowering our gifts, guiding our preaching, sustaining our service, and guiding our mission strategy. Far from an abstract doctrine, Easter's victory invites practical engagement: it fuels compassion ministries, undergirds spiritual warfare, inspires creative evangelism, and infuses leadership with servant-heart resilience. As we examine each facet of ministry in the light of the empty tomb, may we discover in resurrection power the strength and wisdom to persevere, the boldness to proclaim, and the compassion to serve in ways that reflect Christ's triumph over sin and death.

8.1 Rooting Ministry in Resurrection Identity

8.1.1 Union with the Risen Christ as Foundation

Ministry that bears lasting fruit flows from an unbroken union with the risen Lord. Paul illustrates this union by describing baptism as a participation in Christ's death and raising: "Do you not know that all of us who have been baptized into Christ Jesus were baptized into his death?… so that we too might walk in newness of life" (Romans 6:3–4). This oneness with Christ establishes the minister's identity—no longer defined by past failures or worldly accolades but by the reality of being "in Christ" (Galatians 2:20). When leaders grasp their incorporation into the risen life, ministry becomes an overflow of Christ's own power rather than mere human effort. This grounding protects against two extremes: pride that elevates personal gifting above God's grace, and shame that diminishes service due to past shortcomings. Instead, ministers stand secure in a Savior who has triumphed over death and remains the source of our life and service (Colossians 3:1–4). Ongoing spiritual disciplines—prayer, Scripture meditation, and communion—sustain this union, ensuring that every sermon, prayer meeting, and outreach effort radiates the presence of the risen Savior.

8.1.2 Ministering from Newness of Life

Because Christ is alive, those who serve Him are empowered to minister in radical newness of life. Paul exhorts believers to consider themselves "dead to sin and alive to God in Christ Jesus" (Romans 6:11), demonstrating that the Christian's daily experience encompasses both dying to self-centered impulses and rising to fruitful service. This new creation perspective (2 Corinthians 5:17) shifts the focus from merely avoiding moral failure to actively embodying resurrection virtues—mercy, compassion, and hope—in a world still bound by despair. In practical terms, this means approaching outreach not as a duty but as a joyful expression of new life: feeding the hungry, comforting the afflicted, and proclaiming Good News with the confidence that death has lost its sting (1 Corinthians 15:55–57). Ministries shaped by newness of life resist burnout because they draw on inexhaustible resources of grace rather than on personal stamina. By continually relying on resurrection power, ministers model for their congregations how to live free from the old self and empowered for kingdom service.

8.1.3 Witness of Transformed Character

The most compelling sermon often comes not from pulpit eloquence but from a life marked by transformed character. Paul identifies the fruit of the Spirit—love, joy, peace, patience, kindness, goodness, faithfulness, gentleness, self-control—as evidence of Christ's resurrection life at work (Galatians 5:22–23). When ministers and laypeople alike exhibit these qualities amid adversity—extending grace to difficult colleagues, maintaining joy amid financial struggle, or showing gentleness under criticism—they embody a living testimony to the power of Easter. Integrity, in particular, becomes a sermon of its own: honest dealings in administration, transparency in financial reporting, and faithfulness in small tasks underscore that resurrection faith is not compartmentalized but permeates every aspect of life (2 Corinthians 8:21). Communities that prize character transformation over mere numerical growth cultivate maturity that withstands trials and nurtures healthy discipleship. In this way, a resurrection-shaped ethos of integrity and virtue becomes the church's most persuasive evangelistic tool.

8.1.4 Resilience in Ministry Trials

Ministry inevitably encounters trials—opposition, fatigue, personal struggles—that test the resolve of even the most gifted leaders. Yet the same power that raised Christ from the dead equips ministers to endure and flourish amid hardship. Paul's testimony to Timothy—that "the Lord stood by me and strengthened me" when he was abandoned (2 Timothy 4:17)—models how the risen Lord accompanies His servants in their darkest hours. Ministers fortified by resurrection power view trials as refining fires rather than insurmountable obstacles (1 Peter 1:6–7), trusting that God works all things for good for those who are called according to His purpose

(Romans 8:28). Support structures such as mentoring relationships, peer prayer partnerships, and sabbath rhythms provide practical means for sustaining resilience. When congregations celebrate narratives of perseverance and divine faithfulness, they encourage all members to trust in resurrection presence during seasons of discouragement. Ultimately, resilience in ministry emerges not from stoic self-reliance but from resting in the enduring power of the risen Christ.

8.2 Spirit-Empowerment and Gifts in Ministry

8.2.1 Laying on of Hands and Impartation

The practice of impartation—symbolized by the apostles' laying on of hands—demonstrates that ministry flows from Christ's sovereign gifts rather than human ambition (Acts 6:6; 8:17). When elders or apostolic figures pray over emerging ministers, they enact a biblical pattern of divine commissioning, signaling that the Holy Spirit authorizes and empowers for specific tasks. This rite underscores the church's intergenerational continuity: connections to Christ's first apostles remain alive through Spirit-connected networks of mentorship and oversight. Impartation ceremonies remind recipients that their authority originates in the risen Lord and that accountability to the Body is integral to healthy ministry. By regularly reaffirming callings through communal prayer, churches foster unity and shared vision, ensuring that gift-ministry serves the common good rather than personal agendas (Ephesians 4:11–12). Empowered through these acts of laying on of hands, ministers embark on their service journey grounded in divine commission and communal support.

8.2.2 Charismatic Gifts in Service

The Charismatic Renewal highlighted the ongoing availability of spiritual gifts—healing, prophecy, tongues—undergirded by resurrection authority. The Apostle Paul catalogs these manifestations in 1 Corinthians 12, emphasizing that "there are varieties of gifts, but the same Spirit" (v. 4) distributes them "for the common good" (v. 7). When health-care chaplains pray for the sick, expecting supernatural restoration, they step into a lineage that traces back to Peter's shadow healing (Acts 5:15). Prophetic insights in counseling sessions can bring comfort and direction, echoing the risen Lord's role as Shepherd-Prophet. Yet Paul also warns that gifts must operate in love (chapter 13) and be ordered for edification (chapter 14). Training in biblical gift-operational guidelines—such as ensuring interpretation accompanies tongues, or that prophetic words submit to congregational discernment—guard against excess and misuse. Charismatic gifts flourish when anchored in sound theology and pastoral sensitivity, offering vibrant avenues for resurrection power to impact communities.

8.2.3 Operation of Grace Gifts

Paul distinguishes grace gifts—apostles, prophets, evangelists, pastors, teachers—as bestowed "according to the measure of Christ's gift" (Ephesians 4:7). These roles exist not for personal exaltation but "for equipping the saints for the work of ministry, for building up the body of Christ" (Ephesians 4:12). Grace-driven ministry emphasizes service and humility, mirroring Christ's self-emptying (Philippians 2:5–8). In practice, this means validating emerging voices—encouraging new prophets or evangelists while ensuring doctrinal fidelity—so that a culture of mutual edification thrives. Grace gifts call the church to balance visionary innovation with pastoral care, blending pioneering outreach with nurturing discipleship. By maintaining structures that identify, train, and deploy grace ministers, congregations experience exponential growth in both depth and breadth. Resurrection motivation infuses these ministries with zeal, as servers recognize that their calling extends Christ's resurrected presence in tangible ways.

8.2.4 Discernment and Oversight of Spiritual Gifts

Given the variety of gifts, apostolic oversight and communal discernment become essential to ensure that Spirit-given ministries align with Christ's mission. The Apostle John urges believers to "test the spirits… whether they are from God" (1 John 4:1), while Paul instructs that love and order guide gift expressions (1 Corinthians 14:40). Churches establish discernment teams—comprising seasoned leaders and theological advisors—to evaluate emerging ministries, ensuring both doctrinal soundness and relational harmony. Regular gift assessments and coaching sessions help ministers refine their practice, address blind spots, and celebrate successes. This collaborative approach prevents fragmentation—where competing gift ministries vie for prominence—and fosters an environment where every gift serves the Body's unity and mission. By coupling prayerful discernment with clear accountability, the church honors the risen Lord's authority and safeguards the integrity of resurrection-empowered service.

8.3 Preaching and Teaching with Resurrection Authority

8.3.1 Proclaiming Christ Crucified and Risen

The heart of apostolic proclamation is encapsulated in 1 Corinthians 15:1–4: "I delivered to you as of first importance what I also received: that Christ died… was buried… and was raised on the third day." Preaching anchored in these facts carries the authority of the empty tomb. When pastors proclaim Christ's death and resurrection with clarity and conviction, they reenact the earliest kerygma that fueled the church's explosive growth. Christ's resurrection validates every aspect of the gospel message—His identity as Son of God, His atoning death, and His victory over death. Preaching that begins with resurrection deflates competing worldviews, for no other belief system claims authentic conquest of the grave. Such proclamation invites hearers to respond to the living Savior, not merely to a distant historical figure. In every sermon, the central question becomes: "Do you believe in the risen Christ?"—an inquiry that catalyzes life change.

8.3.2 Expository Teaching that Unfolds Easter Themes

Jesus Himself "beginning with Moses and all the Prophets… interpreted in all the Scriptures the things concerning himself" (Luke 24:27). Expository teaching that systematically unpacks resurrection motifs throughout the Bible—Genesis 3's proto-evangelium, Jonah's three days, Psalm 16's no-decay promise—equips congregations to read all Scripture through an Easter lens. Sermon series on Romans 6–8 or 1 Corinthians 15 dive deep into theological and practical implications of resurrection life. Small-group curricula that guide participants through key passages foster lay mastery of resurrection theology, creating a congregation of informed disciples. When teaching emphasizes Scriptural coherence—that every promise finds fulfillment in Easter—the church's faith anchors in divine reliability rather than subjective experience. This robust biblical foundation cultivates resilience in doubt and precision in doctrine.

8.3.3 Homiletical Applications for Daily Life

Preaching that bridges resurrection truth with everyday challenges ensures that sermons move from the pulpit into living rooms and workplaces. Illustrations might connect Romans 6's call to "consider yourselves dead to sin" with overcoming destructive habits, or tie 2 Corinthians 4:10–11's "always carrying in the body the death of Jesus" to persevering through personal crises. Handouts offering reflection questions and action steps help congregants translate Sunday insights into Monday decisions. Prayer stations after sermons allow individuals to receive impromptu prayer, marrying proclamation with personal encounter. Over time, the congregation internalizes a dynamic pattern: hear the resurrection message, apply it to life, and testify to its power. This integrated approach transforms Christianity from a weekly ritual into a radical way of life.

8.3.4 Encouraging Transformational Response

Calls to respond in worship services should flow naturally from resurrection proclamation. When the invitation is framed around Romans 8:11—"if the Spirit of him who raised Jesus from the dead dwells in you…"—respondents understand they step into the very power that raised Christ. Including testimonies of individuals who have experienced resurrection breakthrough (healing from addiction, reconciliation of broken relationships) grounds invitations in tangible reality. Prayer ministry teams standing by after services extend personal ministry to those moved by the sermon. Follow-up care calls or texts ensure that initial responses mature into lasting discipleship. By weaving transformational response opportunities into every service, churches foster environments where Easter conversions become lifelong journeys of growth.

8.4 Healing, Deliverance, and Compassion Ministries

8.4.1 Biblical Foundations for Healing Ministry

Scripture repeatedly associates Christ's healing acts with the inauguration of God's kingdom. Mark 16:17–18 links faith in the risen Lord to signs such as laying hands on the sick for healing. The Epistle of James exhorts believers to "call the elders… and let them pray over him, anointing him with oil in the name of the Lord" for restoration (James 5:14). Jesus' own words—"your faith has made you well" (Mark 5:34)—highlight the interplay of divine grace and human trust. Churches that integrate healing ministries in their care structures affirm that resurrection life brings physical as well as spiritual renewal. Training teams in compassionate presence, basic prayer techniques, and appropriate referral to professional care ensures holistic ministry. By continually returning to biblical model of healing, churches maintain credibility and theological coherence in their compassionate outreach.

8.4.2 Intercessory Prayer and Spiritual Warfare

Ephesians 6:12–18 presents spiritual warfare as "wrestling not against flesh and blood" but against principalities and powers. Intercessory prayer, then, becomes a frontline engagement against demonic forces that hinder human flourishing.

Resurrection authority—Christ's triumph over death—forms the basis for binding satanic strongholds and loosing gospel freedom (Matthew 18:18). Churches host dedicated prayer gatherings, sometimes called "war rooms," where believers plead resurrection power for cities, nations, and individuals. Prayer strategies combine biblical lament, confession, praise, and petition, reflecting the full scope of Christ's victory. Deliverance ministries—conducted with pastoral oversight—offer freedom to those oppressed by spiritual forces (Luke 4:18). By grounding spiritual warfare in the Resurrection, believers avoid sensationalism and remain anchored in the authority of the risen Christ.

8.4.3 Deliverance of Captives

Luke 4:18's promise that Jesus "proclaimed liberty to the captives" echoes throughout deliverance ministries. Inner healing and deliverance courses guide participants in addressing deep-rooted wounds—abuse, rejection, generational curses—through prayer and pastoral counsel. Safe-space groups provide confidentiality and mutual support, ensuring that breakthroughs in freedom lead to ongoing discipleship rather than relapse. Ministers trained in biblical deliverance discernment (1 John 4:1) facilitate sessions that integrate confession, forgiveness, and renunciation of ungodly influences. Pastoral care structures—mentoring relationships, support groups, professional referrals—accompany individuals through the full arc of deliverance. When captives experience genuine freedom, these testimonies powerfully attest to the risen Lord's capacity to break every chain.

8.4.4 Compassionate Presence in Suffering Communities

Easter compassion extends beyond individual healing to collective solidarity with the marginalized. Churches establish outreach to homeless shelters, refugee camps, and inner-city neighborhoods, bringing not only food and clothing but also the proclamation of hope in Christ's resurrection. Mobile outreach teams—equipped with prayer tents and medical volunteers—embody compassion as co-suffering presence, echoing Jesus' incarnational ministry (Matthew 25:35–40).

Partnerships with NGOs and social services multiply impact, ensuring sustainable solutions for poverty, abuse, and injustice. Training in trauma-informed care equips volunteers to respond with sensitivity and grace. Compassionate presence becomes a living sermon, illustrating that Easter compassion engages both spiritual and material dimensions of human need.

8.5 Evangelism and Church Growth by Resurrection Power

8.5.1 Evangelistic Lifestyle for Every Believer

Acts 1:8's promise of Spirit power for witness applies not only to apostles but to every follower of Jesus. An evangelistic lifestyle entails weaving gospel conversations into daily routines—workplace, gym, coffee shop—sharing testimonies of personal transformation and resurrection hope (Philippians 1:27). Churches conduct "resurrection storytelling" workshops that train members to craft concise, authentic testimonies highlighting how Jesus' victory over sin and death changed their lives. Prayer walking neighborhoods and prayer breakfasts for business leaders invite divine appointments. By normalizing gospel sharing as an outgrowth of new life, congregations cultivate cultures where every member participates in the Great Commission. This everyday witness seeds church growth organically, reflecting the pattern of Acts where "the Lord added to their number day by day those who were being saved" (Acts 2:47).

8.5.2 Planting Resurrection Communities

Acts 2:47's depiction of daily additions to the church models a multiplication mindset. Church-planting teams commit to launching new gatherings that prioritize resurrection preaching, Spirit-dependence, and relational evangelism. Contextualization ensures that each plant resonates culturally—adapting worship style, language, and ministries to local contexts while maintaining core Easter truths. Sending churches provide coaching, funding, and prayer cover, reflecting Ephesians 4:16's vision of churches joined and held together. Multiplication pipelines—through training, mentorship, and resource networks—enable exponential growth. New congregations replicate the DNA of resurrection ministry: robust proclamation, compassionate service, and Spirit-empowered witness. This movement of planting communities extends the reach of Easter hope to unreached neighborhoods and peoples.

8.5.3 Discipling New Believers to Risen Life

Following conversion, new believers require formation in resurrection identity and practice. Matthew 28:19–20's command to "teach them to observe all that I have commanded you" involves grounding disciples in Romans 6's truth of dying and rising with Christ and in Galatians 2:20's reality of Christ living in us. New member classes focus on these core passages, helping novices internalize resurrection vocabulary and rhythms—prayer, Scripture, sacrament. Mentorship relationships match each newcomer with seasoned disciple-makers, providing accountability and modeling. Service opportunities—hospitality, outreach, worship—integrate new believers into Body life, confirming their gifts and calling. Discipleship pathways track spiritual growth by fruit of the Spirit and missional engagement, ensuring that initial enthusiasm matures into lifelong devotion.

8.5.4 Strategic Missions with Easter Focus

International mission endeavors grounded in resurrection theology integrate proclamation with compassionate service. Short-term teams combine evangelistic events with feeding programs, medical camps, and construction projects, demonstrating holistic gospel care. Long-term partnerships with indigenous churches ensure that national leaders spearhead follow-up, avoiding dependency and fostering local ownership. Digital missions—radio broadcasts, podcasts, social media campaigns—share Easter messages to billions who cannot enter physical gatherings. Metrics for success include not only conversions and church plants but also improvements in educational attainment, health outcomes, and justice indicators, reflecting the comprehensive renewal that Easter heralds. Strategic mission plans anchored in resurrection power mobilize resources, personnel, and prayer for maximum impact among unreached peoples.

8.6 Leadership Development and Team Empowerment

8.6.1 Servant-Leadership Modeled on the Risen Shepherd

After Peter's denial and restoration, Jesus asked him thrice, "Do you love me?" and commissioned him to "feed my sheep" (John 21:15–17). This paradigm of servant-leadership—love preceding authority—shapes training for ministry leaders. Leaders learn that influence flows from demonstrated care rather than hierarchical power. Seminaries and leadership institutes integrate modules on Christ's pastoral heart, emphasizing listening, empathy, and humility. Leadership retreats incorporate exercises in foot-washing and servant tasks, reinforcing the call to serve "as the Son of Man came not to be served but to serve" (Matthew 20:28). These experiences cultivate a leadership culture where status measurements give way to sacrificial service, mirroring the resurrected Lord's heart for His flock.

8.6.2 Mentoring and Multiplication of Leaders

Paul's charge to Timothy—"Entrust to faithful men who will be able to teach others also" (2 Timothy 2:2)—articulates a multiplication model for leadership. Churches implement mentoring cohorts pairing seasoned pastors with emerging leaders, focusing on theological formation, pastoral skills, and spiritual disciplines. Apprenticeship projects engage mentees in preaching, pastoral visits, and team leadership, providing experiential learning under supervision. Milestone reviews assess character, competence, and calling before advancing to greater responsibilities. This intentional pipeline ensures leadership continuity and prevents burnout by distributing responsibilities. As mentees themselves become mentors, the cycle of multiplication honors the Great Commission's generational mandate.

8.6.3 Building Resurrection-Centered Teams

Healthy ministry teams share a common vision shaped by Easter values—unity, hope, compassion—and commit to collaborative practices. Team charters articulate mission statements rooted in Christ's resurrection purpose, aligning goals and expectations. Weekly worship huddles—brief gatherings of prayer, Scripture reading, and mutual encouragement—recenter teams on the risen Lord's presence. Conflict-resolution protocols based on Matthew 18's reconciliation steps maintain relational health. Celebrating answered prayers and ministry milestones fosters shared joy and collective memory of God's faithfulness. When teams innovate—through "resurrection brainstorming"—they seek Spirit-led solutions rather than defaulting to familiar methods. Such rhythms embed resurrection DNA in organizational culture, enabling teams to flourish under pressure and pivot creatively in changing contexts.

8.6.4 Accountability and Care in Ministry Teams

Ministry can exact a heavy toll on leaders' emotional, spiritual, and relational resources. Establishing confidential "Safe Space" groups where leaders share struggles and pray for one another provides crucial mutual support. Accountability agreements—outlining confidentiality, prayer support, and corrective feedback—create environments of trust. Pastoral care structures offering counseling referrals, sabbath scheduling, and sabbatical leaves safeguard mental health. Peer supervision teams and board oversight ensure ethical conduct and prevent abuses of power. By institutionalizing care and accountability, churches honor both the risen Lord's desire for healthy leaders and the communal responsibility to protect and restore those who serve Him.

8.7 Worship and Sacraments as Ministry Gateways

8.7.1 Eucharistic Ministry and Table Fellowship

The Lord's Supper stands at the intersection of worship and ministry. Beyond Sunday liturgy, mobile Eucharist teams visit hospitals, prisons, and care homes, extending resurrection presence to those unable to attend services. Training lay ministers to administer bread and cup ensures that tables of grace proliferate in homes, venues, and public spaces. Accompanying pastoral prayers at the table offer opportunities for healing, confession, and commissioning. Through Eucharistic ministry, believers experience the risen Christ tangibly and are sent forth to embody His love in word and deed.

8.7.2 Baptism as Commissioning into Service

Every baptism service integrates celebration with commissioning: new believers publicly proclaim their union with Christ's death and resurrection and the congregation commits to support their spiritual journey. Godparent or sponsor systems pair each new believer with a mentor who helps interpret baptismal meaning, identify gifts, and connect them to service opportunities. Baptismal testimonies link personal narratives to Easter's grand story, inspiring the church toward greater faithfulness. Follow-up programs— baptism classes, welcome lunches, small-group integration— ensure that the baptized are nurtured and deployed for ministry.

8.7.3 The Role of Worship in Empowering Ministry

Worship services that incorporate times of prophetic song, spontaneous prayer, and declarations of Easter truths prime hearts for ministry engagement. Intercessory worship segments invite congregants to pray for specific ministries— outreach teams, compassion projects, global partnerships— integrating prayer and mission. Activation moments, where gifted laypeople are invited forward for prayer and commissioning, snowball ministry involvement. Worship leadership development programs equip singers, instrumentalists, and tech teams to see their roles as frontline ministry. By embedding ministry activation into worship, churches blur the line between "Sunday spectators" and "week-long ministers."

8.7.4 Pastoral Care through Sacramental Rites

Sacramental rites—anointing with oil (James 5:14), confession and absolution, marriage and child-dedication services—serve as portals for pastoral care. Anointing ceremonies often combine prayer for healing with personal ministry, bringing resurrection compassion to the fore. Confession services rooted in Easter forgiveness offer avenues for restoration and renewal. Marriage and home-blessing rituals invoke resurrection promises over families, forging spiritual resilience. By weaving sacraments into care pathways, pastors ensure that God's grace touches every season of life, from suffering to celebration.

8.8 Sustaining Ministry Through Rest and Renewal

8.8.1 Sabbath Rhythms for Ministers

Even our Lord sought intentional withdrawal: "Come away to a desolate place and rest a while" (Mark 6:31). Ministers honor Sabbath rhythms by scheduling weekly days off—complete disengagement from emails, calls, and ministry tasks—to rest in resurrection assurance. Collaborative planning among staff and volunteers ensures ministry continuity without overloading any individual. Regular Sabbath fosters creativity, spiritual refreshment, and family bonds, preventing burnout and sustaining long-term service. Such rhythms testify that even the Son of Man restored His strength by resting in the Father's presence.

8.8.2 Retreats for Refreshment in Resurrection Presence

Multi-day retreats at the beginning or midpoint of the year offer extended sabbatical-style renewal. Retreat centers—situated in natural settings that echo creation's groan and promise of restoration (Romans 8:22)—provide solitude, guided prayer walks, and times of corporate worship. Retreats blend teaching on resurrection themes with extended silence, sacramental liturgies, and artistic reflection. Pastors emerge from these retreats renewed in vision and vitality. Post-retreat debriefs integrate insights into ministry strategy, ensuring that God's voice in silence translates into congregational impact.

8.8.3 Peer Support and Restorative Communities

Nothing sustains ministry like authentic friendships of mutual care. Peer support groups among clerks, deacons, or pastors meet regularly to share joys, confess struggles, and pray for one another. Restorative communities—gathered around shared spiritual disciplines and artistic expression—create safe spaces where vulnerability is honored. Instead of competition, leaders cultivate camaraderie marked by empathy and encouragement. These bonds function as spiritual lifelines when ministry storms rage, reminding us that resurrection community transcends programmatic engagement.

8.8.4 Avoiding Burnout: Lessons from Peter's Restoration

Peter's own journey—from brash denial to humbled restoration by the charcoal fire (John 18; 21)—offers a paradigm for recovery after failure. Churches institute "failure recovery" protocols: safe confession circles, restorative liturgies modeled on Psalm 51, and structured mentorship in which restored leaders rediscover calling. Emphasizing identity in Christ over performance liberates ministers from the tyranny of perfectionism. Regular "pulse checks" and 360° feedback guard against toxic culture, ensuring that struggles lead to deeper dependence on the risen Lord. By learning from Peter's restoration, ministry teams cultivate resilience and grace in the face of inevitable stumbles.

8.9 Measuring Fruit: Evaluating Resurrection Impact

8.9.1 Spiritual Growth Indicators

True ministry fruit transcends attendance and budget figures. Spiritual growth manifests in deeper community life—small-group participation, prayer meeting attendance, and qualitative testimonies of transformation. Congregational surveys assessing frequency of personal devotions, experience of God's presence, and fruit of the Spirit (Galatians 5:22–23) provide insights into discipleship health. Collecting personal stories in "resurrection journals" captures the intangible yet essential impact of Easter truth in everyday lives. Church leaders use these data to tailor ministries, ensuring that programs foster genuine spiritual vitality.

8.9.2 Community Transformation Metrics

Resurrection compassion seeks justice and renewal in local contexts. Tracking metrics such as meals distributed, jobs created through vocational programs, and educational gains in community schools paints a picture of tangible impact. Partnering with local NGOs to measure changes in poverty rates, public health indices, and crime statistics demonstrates that Easter outreach extends beyond spiritual conversion to holistic community well-being. Publishing annual impact reports that highlight both statistical outcomes and narrative case studies celebrates God's redemptive work and encourages continued partnership.

8.9.3 Kingdom Multiplication and Continuity

The early church grew as "the Lord added to their number day by day" (Acts 2:47). Measuring kingdom multiplication involves tracking new disciples baptized, new small groups launched, and new church plants established. Leadership pipelines—evaluating number of mentored leaders and multiplied ministry teams—ensure that growth is sustainable. Success is not merely numeric but relational: each new believer is integrated into discipleship pathways and gift-based service opportunities. By valuing multiplication alongside depth, churches maintain balance between expansion and maturity.

8.9.4 Aligning Outcomes with Resurrection Objectives

Regular strategic reviews help ministries stay anchored in Easter purposes rather than slipping into programmatic inertia. Leadership teams convene to assess whether activities align with core objectives: proclaiming Christ's death and resurrection, equipping disciples, and serving communities. Programs that drift from resurrection focus are reimagined or retired. Celebratory gatherings—where successes are attributed to Christ's power—reinforce the centrality of resurrection. This cyclical realignment ensures that ministry remains vibrant, faithful, and impactful, always emerging from the heartbeat of Easter power.

Conclusion Resurrection power permeates every facet of Christian ministry, from the inner formation of leaders to the global outreach that brings hope to unreached communities. When rooted in union with the risen Christ and empowered by the Spirit's gifts, ministry transcends mere technique, becoming an authentic expression of Easter's triumph. Healing and deliverance flow from divine authority, compassion springs from solidarity with the suffering, and evangelistic fervor ignites in quotidian contexts as believers testify to life beyond death. Leadership marked by servanthood and resilience, worship woven with sacraments, and community sustained by rhythms of rest all bear witness to the risen Lord. As churches measure their fruit, may they celebrate not human ingenuity but Christ's transformative power at work. Ultimately, the church's calling is to advance Jesus' victory over sin and death into every corner of society, confident that the same power that raised Him from the grave continues to renew individuals, congregations, and nations until the day He returns. May we, by grace, live and minister as resurrection people, heralding the good news that Christ is risen indeed.

Chapter 9: Eschatological Hope— Firstfruits to Final Fulfillment

The resurrection of Jesus Christ stands at the heart of Christian hope, promising not only individual renewal but the ultimate renewal of all creation. When Christ rose from the dead, He became the forerunner of new life, the guarantee that death has been conquered and that God's redemptive purposes will reach their consummation. This event inaugurates an "already-but-not-yet" reality in which believers live empowered by resurrection life now, even as they anticipate the full revelation of that life at Christ's return. Throughout redemptive history, God has pointed forward to this climactic moment—from the Old Testament feasts of firstfruits to the prophetic visions of universal restoration— revealing a future where every tear is wiped away, and death is no more. In this chapter, we will trace the trajectory from Christ's firstfruits rise through the present unfolding of the kingdom and toward the final restoration of heaven and earth. Along the way, we will explore how resurrection hope shapes ethical urgency, drives compassionate ministry, frames the church's mission, and anchors our ultimate destiny. May this exploration kindle fresh awe and resolve, as we live in the light of Easter dawn while looking forward to the day when resurrection hope becomes final fulfillment.

9.1 The Firstfruits of Resurrection

The concept of firstfruits provides a vital theological anchor, linking Christ's resurrection to God's covenantal calendar and to the hope of future harvest. In ancient Israel, the first sheaf of the barley harvest was presented to the Lord as a sign that the rest of the harvest was secure (Leviticus 23:10–11). Paul seizes this imagery in 1 Corinthians 15:20–23, declaring Jesus "the firstfruits of those who have fallen asleep," thus guaranteeing that all who belong to Him will likewise be raised. This metaphor underscores both precedence—Christ rose first—and guarantee—the remainder of the harvest will follow. As firstfruits, Christ's resurrection inaugurates a new creation, signaling that the old order is passing away and that the new is breaking in. Early Christian liturgy reflected this link: Easter celebrations led directly into Pentecost, the feast of weeks, itself tied to the firstfruits offering of the barley (Exodus 34:22). The outpouring of the Spirit on Pentecost (Acts 2:17–21) becomes the firstfruits of the Spirit, confirming that resurrection life now courses through the Body of Christ. Thus, resurrection firstfruits bridge past promise, present experience, and future consummation, forming the backbone of Christian eschatological hope.

9.1.1 Pauline Imagery of Firstfruits

Paul's usage of firstfruits language carries profound weight for understanding Christian hope. In 1 Corinthians 15:20, the phrase "Christ has been raised from the dead, the firstfruits of those who have fallen asleep" positions Christ's resurrection as both inaugural event and foretaste of general resurrection. By paralleling agricultural customs—wherein the initial offering signified the full harvest—Paul assures believers that their own bodily resurrection is as certain as Christ's. The sequence "Christ the firstfruits, then at his coming those who belong to him" (v. 23) preserves the anticipation of a future collective awakening. Furthermore, in Romans 8:23, Paul describes believers receiving "the firstfruits of the Spirit," indicating that the indwelling Spirit is a present down payment of the ultimate redemption. These twin firstfruits—Christ's resurrection and Spirit's presence—anchor Christian life in both past accomplishment and future expectation. Paul's imagery thus weaves together personal transformation, corporate destiny, and cosmic renewal, encouraging believers to live in resurrection power with eyes fixed on the harvest to come.

9.1.2 Old Testament Roots and New-Covenant Fulfillment

The festival of firstfruits emerges in Exodus 23:16 and Numbers 28:26 as a celebration of the barley harvest, acknowledging God's provision and sovereignty over the land. Leviticus 23:10–14 mandates that the priest "present a sheaf of the firstfruits of your harvest to the LORD," which would initiate the full grain offering to follow. The prophetic promise in Joel 2:28–29 anticipates a new outpouring: "And it shall come to pass afterward, that I will pour out my Spirit... and I will show wonders in the heavens and on the earth." Peter applies this prophecy to Pentecost (Acts 2:16–21), linking the feast of weeks—which occurs fifty days after firstfruits—with the Spirit's descent upon the church. Thus, the Old Testament feasts form a chronological and thematic blueprint: firstfruits offering, harvest affirmation, and covenant empowerment. Jesus' resurrection fulfills the firstfruits, inaugurating the new Israel, while Pentecost fulfills Joel's promise, equipping the new covenant people. The church stands at the intersection of these festivals, living between the initial harvest sign and the anticipated fullness. Understanding these roots enriches eschatological hope, revealing that Easter and Pentecost are covenantal bookends around which redemptive life unfolds.

9.1.3 Believers as Firstfruits in New Creation

James 1:18 deepens the firstfruits motif by declaring believers "a kind of firstfruits of his creatures." This designation confers both honor and responsibility: as the pioneering yield of God's creative action in Christ, believers embody the reality of new creation even now. Peter echoes this sentiment in 1 Peter 1:3–5, describing a "new birth into a living hope" through Jesus' resurrection, guaranteeing an inheritance that is imperishable and undefiled. As firstfruits, Christians participate in the initial phase of God's cosmic renewal, tasting the life that will one day permeate all creation. This identity shapes communal ethics: those who are firstfruits invest in holistic transformation, modeling kingdom life in the present. Churches, in turn, nurture this status by discipleship practices that emphasize future orientation—baptism into new life, eucharistic anticipation of the marriage feast, and spiritual gifts employed for edification. Thus, the church is called to manifest resurrection life now, foreshadowing the full renewal that awaits.

9.1.4 Pentecost: Firstfruits of the Spirit

The Day of Pentecost marks the climax of firstfruits symbolism when the Holy Spirit is poured out upon the church (Acts 2:1–4). This event occurs during the feast of weeks, itself the culmination of the seven-week countdown from the firstfruits offering of barley. Peter explicitly ties the Spirit's arrival to Joel's prophecy, establishing Pentecost as the firstfruits of the Spirit's work among all nations (Acts 2:17–21). The subsequent signs—signs, wonders, and bold proclamation—provide tangible evidence that resurrection power has broken into the world. Believers experience Spirit baptism as both empowerment for witness (Acts 1:8) and as participation in the life of the risen Christ (Romans 8:11). This firstfruits outpouring equips the church to carry the harvest of souls and to cultivate communities marked by Spirit gifts and fruit. Pentecost thus situates the church at the nexus of resurrection and renewal, commissioning it to extend Easter's victory until every tribe and tongue rejoices in the harvest of new creation.

9.2 Living "Already/Not Yet" Kingdom

Eschatological hope is shaped by the tension between what has been inaugurated and what awaits consummation. Jesus announced the kingdom of God as present in His ministry—"the kingdom of God is in the midst of you" (Luke 17:21)—yet He also spoke of its future fullness. This inaugurated eschatology frames Christian existence: believers live empowered by resurrection life now, while awaiting the day when Christ's reign will be universally acknowledged and all creation restored. New Testament writers articulate this dual reality through "already/not yet" language, urging faithfulness amid imperfection and anticipation of glory. This tension propels mission and shapes ethical priorities, as the church embodies foretaste of the consummated kingdom. By embracing both dimensions, Christians cultivate resilience to endure suffering, urgency to proclaim the gospel, and gratitude that every step toward justice reflects Easter's coming triumph.

9.2.1 Inaugurated Eschatology in Jesus' Teachings

Jesus' teaching inaugurated the kingdom with both present power and future promise. He proclaimed, "Repent, for the kingdom of heaven is at hand" (Matthew 4:17), signaling that in His words and deeds—healings, exorcisms, restoration of sight—the age to come had broken into the present. Parables such as the mustard seed and the leaven (Matthew 13:31–33) illustrate the kingdom's hidden beginnings and its inevitable expansion. Yet Jesus also warned of a future day of judgment and accountability (Matthew 25:31–46), teaching His disciples to live in expectant readiness. His life exemplified this tension: He enjoyed communion with the Father through prayer (Luke 5:16) even as He faced the anticipation of His suffering and return (Luke 22:69). This inaugurated eschatology empowers believers to engage in kingdom work—compassion, justice, and proclamation—while maintaining the hope of final consummation. The church, following this model, prays "Your kingdom come" (Matthew 6:10), embodying present reality and future yearning in one breath.

9.2.2 New Testament Voices on "Already/Not Yet"

Paul and Peter offer the clearest articulations of the "already/not yet" paradigm. Paul speaks of the Spirit as "the firstfruits" of our inheritance (Romans 8:23), reminding believers that while they enjoy new-creation life now, they await full redemption. In 1 Corinthians 13:12, he contrasts "now" prophetic vision with "then" face-to-face communion, urging maturity in faith amid partial understanding. Peter, writing to persecuted Christians, points to "inheritance… kept in heaven" (1 Peter 1:4), calling them to rejoice despite temporal trials. The author of Hebrews anchors hope in Jesus as "the pioneer and perfecter of our faith" (Hebrews 12:2), who suffered before entering His glory. Revelation's visions— present worship in heaven's throne room (Revelation 4–5) alongside future resurrection judgments (Revelation 20) and new creation (Revelation 21)—offer a panoramic view of inaugurated and consummated realities. These voices assure believers that despite the present groaning, God's purposes march inexorably toward fulfillment, and that resurrection life is the engine of this divine progression.

9.2.3 Living Between Two Ages in Daily Practice

The tension of living between ages transforms ethics, worship, mission, and suffering. Ethically, believers are called to "put to death the deeds of the body" by the Spirit (Romans 8:13), embodying kingdom virtues before the world while resisting the values of the passing age. Worship reflects this duality: the Lord's Supper proclaims Christ's death until He comes (1 Corinthians 11:26), merging remembrance with anticipation. Mission gains urgency from the shortness of time: Jesus warned that the harvest is plentiful yet laborers are few (Luke 10:2), urging prompt proclamation. In suffering, Christians "rejoice in hope of the glory of God" (Romans 5:2), finding meaning in pain as a refining process that points to final glory. Community life—hospitality, justice ministries, koinōnia— serves as a miniature new creation, testifying that present relationships anticipate perfected fellowship in the age to come. Thus, daily discipleship becomes a constant negotiation between what is already ours in Christ and what is promised by His return.

9.2.4 Tensions and Triumphs in Ministry Contexts

Ministry leaders navigate complex tensions inherent in inaugurated eschatology. Balancing social engagement with trust in divine sovereignty guards against either complacent quietism or utopian activism. Preaching the future kingdom must avoid escapism by tethering hope to practical compassion and justice. Congregations facing decline or persecution find encouragement in the promise of final resurrection, even as they labor faithfully. Cross-cultural ministries wrestle with contextual adaptation without compromising the universal consummation. Ethical discernment frameworks help leaders apply eschatological hope to emerging moral dilemmas. Yet the triumph lies in witnessing communities that reflect resurrection life: when reconciliation occurs in divided societies, when those released from addiction testify to new-creation transformation, and when gospel advances despite seemingly insurmountable barriers. These triumphs affirm that even amid tensions, resurrection power is at work, advancing God's reign in incremental yet decisive ways.

9.3 Resurrection Body and Final Consummation

The doctrine of the resurrection body provides a cornerstone for Christian anthropology and eschatology. Paul's extended treatment in 1 Corinthians 15:35–58 clarifies that resurrection bodies will be imperishable, glorious, powerful, and spiritual, in contrast to natural, perishable flesh. Christ's own post-resurrection appearances—eating broiled fish (Luke 24:42–43), inviting Thomas to touch His wounds (John 20:27)—demonstrate both continuity with physical life and transformative qualities. Early church theologians, from Justin Martyr to Augustine, reflected on how death's vanquish yields bodies suited for eternal communion with God. This teaching shapes Christian views of birth, aging, illness, and death, affirming that physical life matters and that our bodies participate in divine redemption. By anticipating bodies free from corruption yet bearing Christ's victorious marks, believers gain fresh perspective on present suffering and steward creation in light of future glory.

9.3.1 Nature of the Resurrection Body

Paul addresses skeptics in Corinth who questioned bodily resurrection by asking, "How are the dead raised? With what sort of body do they come?" (1 Corinthians 15:35). He responds by explaining that just as a seed must die to bring forth new plant life, so the resurrection body arises from the perishable to embody imperishable life (vv. 36–44). This body is "sown a natural body; it is raised a spiritual body" (v. 44), indicating a transformation that transcends current physical limitations without negating physicality altogether. Christ's risen body—recognizable yet transformed—serves as the prototype: He passed through locked doors (John 20:19), appeared unannounced, yet retained the marks of crucifixion as emblems of victory (John 20:27). The resurrection body will reflect the fullness of God's presence: luminous, powerful, and suited for life in a renewed creation. This doctrine affirms the goodness of creation, upholds human dignity against dualistic contempt, and anchors hope in more than disembodied existence.

9.3.2 New Heavens and New Earth

Revelation 21:1–4 unveils the culmination of creation's redemption: "a new heaven and a new earth, for the first heaven and the first earth had passed away." Isaiah 65:17–25 and 2 Peter 3:13 similarly portray a cosmic renewal where pain and death are no more. Resurrection's implications extend beyond personal immortality to the healing of all creation, fulfilling God's original intention for a harmonious world (Genesis 1–2). This vision compels Christian environmental stewardship, as believers partner with God's redemptive work in creation, recognizing that present care participates in future consummation (Romans 8:19–21). The new Jerusalem's description—walls of jasper, streets of gold, river of life, and tree of healing—symbolizes perfection and continuous communion with God (Revelation 21:10–27; 22:1–5). By anticipating this reality, the church worships and works with eternity in view, ensuring that present actions align with future glory. This cosmic scope magnifies Easter's power, revealing resurrection life as world-transforming.

9.3.3 The New Jerusalem and Dwelling with God

Central to the new creation is the habitation of God with His people: "Behold, the dwelling place of God is with man. He will dwell with them, and they will be his people" (Revelation 21:3). Unlike the tabernacle or temple where God's presence was mediated, the new Jerusalem requires no temple because God and the Lamb are its temple (v. 22). The imagery of a bride-city (v. 2), laid as a foundation with apostles' and tribes' names (v. 14), bridges covenantal promises to eschatological reality. The river of life and tree of life evoke Eden's restoration, indicating perennial sustenance and healing (Revelation 22:1–2). This vision reshapes Christian worship: congregations rehearse heavenly worship patterns—united praise, diversity of peoples, and direct access to God—anticipating the ultimate liturgy. It also frames mission: inviting all to the wedding feast of the Lamb (Revelation 19:9) becomes the church's highest calling. The new Jerusalem thus stands as both goal and template for present communal life.

9.3.4 Baptism and Eucharist as Previews of Consummation

The sacraments function as tangible encounters with resurrection realities. Baptism immerses believers into Christ's death and resurrection (Romans 6:3–4), symbolizing both personal cleansing and corporate participation in the coming resurrection body. The Lord's Supper proclaims the Lord's death and anticipates His coming with the banquet imagery of Revelation 19:9—"Blessed are those who are called to the marriage supper of the Lamb." During the Easter Vigil, baptismal rites and Eucharist intertwine, reenacting salvation history as both retrospective and prospective: looking back to Christ's victory while looking forward to final fulfilment. Liturgical elements—water, oil, bread, wine—become sacramental seals of the promised new creation. By engaging in these practices, the church lives "between the ages," tasting future glory and carrying Easter hope into everyday life. These previews of consummation ground eschatological hope in embodied worship and anticipation.

9.4 Final Judgment: Resurrection for Life and Judgment

The New Testament portrays a final resurrection that will culminate in divine judgment and restoration. Jesus declared that all who are in their graves will hear His voice and come forth, "those who have done good to the resurrection of life, and those who have done evil to the resurrection of judgment" (John 5:28–29). This paired outcome underlines God's holiness and justice, as well as His mercy for the repentant. The parable of the sheep and goats (Matthew 25:31–46) further associates final judgment with tangible acts of compassion, indicating that eschatological accountability encompasses both belief and deeds. Revelation's depiction of two resurrections—first the blessed who reign with Christ, then the rest judged at the Great White Throne—reinforces this duality (Revelation 20:4–6, 11–15). For the church, this teaching shapes both evangelistic urgency and pastoral care, urging proclamation to avert condemnation while offering comfort that resurrection life awaits those in Christ. In this light, Christian mission is both invitation and warning, grounded in resurrection power that conquers sin and death but also respects divine justice.

9.4.1 Jesus' Teachings on Resurrection and Judgment

In John 5:28–29, Jesus explicitly connects resurrection with future judgment, declaring that the voice of the Son of Man will raise all from their graves to either life or condemnation. His parables amplify this message: the Sheep and Goat judgment in Matthew 25 sees the righteous inherit kingdom blessing based on compassionate deeds, while the unprepared face banishment (Matthew 25:31–46). The criteria—feeding the hungry, welcoming strangers, caring for the sick—underscore that faith must manifest in love and service. Jesus' warnings about the narrow way (Matthew 7:13–14) and suddenness of His return (Matthew 24:36–44) drive home the urgency of moral readiness. Yet He also offers assurance: "Whoever believes in the Son has eternal life; but whoever rejects the Son will not see life" (John 3:36). The tension of comfort and warning propels the church's mission: to beckon all toward the risen Lord, who alone initiates resurrection life and final vindication.

9.4.2 Revelation's Two Resurrections

John's Apocalypse unpacks the drama of final resurrection in Revelation 20. The first resurrection gathers martyrs and those faithful to Christ, who "came to life and reigned with Christ a thousand years" (v. 4), an image of blessed intimacy with the risen Lord. Those who partake in this resurrection are called "blessed and holy" (v. 6) because the "second death has no power over them." After the thousand years, the rest of the dead are raised and judged according to their deeds, with death and Hades thrown into the lake of fire (vv. 11–15). This stark contrast underscores both the gracious invitation of resurrection life and the solemn reality of judgment for the unrepentant. Pastoral ministry emerges from this vision, combining the joyful proclamation of eternal fellowship with the sober reminder of divine accountability. Churches equip members to embrace the hope of the first resurrection while sharing the urgency of decision before the last trumpet sounds.

9.4.3 Implications for Christian Hope and Mission

The doctrine of final resurrection and judgment imparts dual impetus to hope-filled evangelism and ethical living. Knowing that Christ will return as Judge—"with wrath and fury to execute judgment" (Isaiah 66:15–16)—inspires urgent proclamation so that as many as possible can receive mercy (James 5:20). At the same time, the assurance of vindication and reward for the faithful fuels endurance among persecuted believers (Revelation 2–3). Ethical imperatives—caring for the poor, advocating for justice—gain eternal significance, contributing to one's testimony before the Great White Throne (Matthew 25:40). Mission strategies integrate invitation to life with service projects that meet tangible needs, embodying the compassion that will characterize final judgment. Pastoral preaching balances the "gospel of grace" with the sobering call to holiness, as James exhorts: "be doers of the word, and not hearers only" (James 1:22). Thus, final resurrection doctrine shapes a holistic ministry that embraces hope and warns of judgment, confident that resurrection power sustains both.

9.5 Triumph Over Death: Eschatological Restoration

The climactic note of Pauline eschatology in 1 Corinthians 15:54–57 bursts forth in triumphant doxology: "Death is swallowed up in victory... thanks be to God, who gives us the victory through our Lord Jesus Christ." This victory over death's sting rescinds evil's claim and secures God's ultimate reign. The taunting question—"O death, where is your victory? O death, where is your sting?"—echoes prophetic assurance (Hosea 13:14) and celebrates God's power to reverse the curse. Early Christians fashioned funeral liturgies around this text, transforming gravesides into Easter festivals. By internalizing this victory, believers face life's final frontier not with despair but with confident expectation. Moreover, Resurrection does not merely abolish death for individuals—it sets in motion the restoration of all things, calling creation itself to join in the anthem of cosmic renewal.

9.5.1 Victory Proclaimed: "Death Is Swallowed Up in Victory"

Paul's exultant statement in 1 Corinthians 15:54 transforms the cross's lament into the trumpet of triumph. When death is swallowed up, its power to separate, despair, and destroy is nullified in the resurrected Christ. This victory shapes Christian funerals, reframing them as temporary farewells en route to everlasting fellowship (1 Thessalonians 4:13–18). Pastoral care for the grieving hinges on this promise, offering comfort that loved ones who die in Christ participate in the first resurrection (Revelation 20:6). Liturgies incorporate Scripture, song, and a memorial meal to anticipate the wedding feast of the Lamb (Revelation 19:9). In daily life, the victory chant bolsters resilience, reminding believers that no sickness, sorrow, or sin can ultimately prevail. Thus, the proclamation of victory becomes the heartbeat of Christian hope and the lens through which all suffering is reframed.

9.5.2 Cosmic Redemption and Creation's Groaning

Paul's cosmic vision in Romans 8:19–23 reveals that "the creation waits with eager longing for the revealing of the sons of God," groaning under bondage to corruption. Resurrection inaugurates this redemption, fulfilling God's original intent for creation to reflect His glory (Genesis 1:26–28). The firstfruits of redemption—the church, the Spirit's outpouring, and resurrected bodies—offer glimpses of a cosmic harvest where storms cease, deserts bloom, and predators lie down with prey (Isaiah 11:6–9). Environmental stewardship thus becomes an act of eschatological solidarity, participating in cosmic redemption rather than mere conservation. Worship that includes creation-care commitments and corporate prayers for the environment resonates with prophetic hopes. As believers work toward justice, reconciliation, and ecological restoration, they embody the forward momentum of resurrection power, anticipating a time when groaning creation will be set free from decay.

9.5.3 Extended Hope: Universal Restoration?

Early theologians such as Irenaeus and Augustine pondered the scope of cosmic restoration—whether God's redemptive purposes would ultimately embrace even all fallen creatures (apokatastasis). Scripture presents tensions: passages such as Colossians 1:20 speak of God "reconciling to himself all things, whether on earth or in heaven," while Revelation 20:15 warns that those not found in the Book of Life face the second death. Contemporary theologians mediate these tensions by affirming God's universal saving will (1 Timothy 2:4) alongside human responsibility and freedom. Pastoral care encourages hope for creation's renewal while upholding the seriousness of divine justice. The church's mission, then, advocates for universal proclamation and honors every person's freedom to embrace or reject the risen Lord. Resurrection hope thus extends to the cosmic horizon while respecting moral agency, inspiring both bold evangelism and humble trust in God's perfect wisdom.

9.6 Living in the Light of Consummation

Awareness of Christ's eventual return imbues Christian living with both urgency and hope. To know that "the end of all things is at hand" (1 Peter 4:7) urges moral vigilance and fervent devotion. The final consummation—when heaven and earth merge, and God dwells with His people—beckons believers to orient their ethical choices accordingly. Jesus' call to watchfulness (Mark 13:33–37) echoes across the ages, reminding disciples that faithful stewardship and readiness are both spiritual disciplines and missional imperatives. Worship services draw upon Revelation's heavenly scenes (Revelation 4–5) to rehearse future praise, infusing present gatherings with celestial wonder. Community rhythms of fasting, confession, and service reflect the dual posture of penitent anticipation and active engagement. Living in this light means pursuing holiness not as legalistic obligation but as spontaneous outpouring of resurrection life, confident that the same Christ who rose from the dead will one day bring all things to glorious completion.

9.6.1 Ethical Urgency and Moral Living

Knowing the final day influences ethical priorities: the inevitability of Christ's coming fuels commitment to justice, compassion, and holiness. James exhorts believers to "be patient... until the coming of the Lord" (James 5:7), likening perseverance to season-bound patience in agricultural harvest. The Beatitudes outline the character traits blessed at consummation—poor in spirit, merciful, pure in heart (Matthew 5:3–12)—indicating that present moral formation aligns with future inheritance. Issues such as economic exploitation, systemic injustice, and environmental abuse gain moral urgency when viewed through the lens of eschatological accountability. Churches develop accountability structures— ethical codes, restorative justice ministries, advocacy teams— that translate final hope into present-day action. Preaching on judgment passages, such as the sheep and goats, moves congregations from apathy to engaged living, ensuring that moral living is not optional but integral to consummated hope.

9.6.2 Worship Shaped by Futuristic Vision

Revelation's visions of unceasing worship—every creature praising the Lamb (Revelation 5:13)—offer templates for congregational liturgy. Elements such as incense, lamps, and processions recall temple worship elevated to cosmic scale. Music can incorporate themes from Revelation's new song (Revelation 5:9) and the victory chorus of resurrection. Iconography—images of the Lamb, the Throne, and the New Jerusalem—adorns worship spaces, orienting hearts to the eternal. The liturgical calendar embeds eschatological texts throughout the year: Advent's longing, Easter's triumph, Christ the King Sunday's cosmic reign. These practices weave future hope into present worship, reminding believers that their gatherings are foretaste of the heavenly assembly. By singing with "a great multitude that no one could number" (Revelation 7:9), the church bridges the divide between earth and heaven.

9.6.3 Mission and Waiting: Acts 1 Model

Before ascending, Jesus commanded His disciples to remain in Jerusalem "until you are clothed with power from on high" (Luke 24:49). They responded by dedicating themselves to prayer and waiting (Acts 1:14), a posture that preceded the Pentecostal outpouring (Acts 2:1–4). This model—waiting in prayer until empowered—frames effective mission: strategic planning followed by Spirit-led launching. Periods of corporate fasting and prayer emphasize dependence, as does centering team retreats on the Scripture's resurrection promises. Waiting cultivates unity and clarifies vision, ensuring mission emerges not from human zeal alone but from Spirit-endued power. When the church balances preparation with proclamation, it echoes the early community's rhythm, activating resurrection momentum for global witness. This dynamic—prayerful waiting followed by vibrant outreach—keeps mission both faithful and fruitful until Christ returns.

9.7 Invitational Horizon: Hope-Filled Evangelism

The crescendo of eschatological hope impels evangelism that offers resurrection life as the ultimate solution to the human predicament. Jesus' declaration, "I am the resurrection and the life; he who believes in me... shall live" (John 11:25–26), frames the gospel as an invitation to personal and cosmic renewal. Evangelistic methods rooted in resurrection hope shift focus from moral chess to life-and-death realities, meeting existential longing with divine promise. Personal testimonies of deliverance resonate with seekers facing death's specter—whether literal or metaphorical. Churches equip believers through "resurrection storytelling" workshops, helping them craft narratives that connect the gospel with everyday experiences of struggle and restoration. Outreach events blend compelling testimonies, creative media, and service projects, demonstrating that Easter hope addresses spiritual, emotional, and material needs. This invitational horizon honors human freedom while presenting Christ's resurrection as the decisive turning point for individuals and societies.

9.7.1 Sharing Resurrection Hope as Life Invitation

Evangelism begins with the proposition that true life transcends the grave. Jesus' words in John 10:10—"I came that they may have life and have it abundantly"—underscore resurrection's transformative scope. Believers share not only doctrinal truths but living encounters, illustrating how resurrection hope sustained them through crises. Neighborhood Bible study groups can be rebranded "Life Groups," emphasizing exploration of resurrection life. Churches host "Easter All Year" seminars, inviting nonbelievers to hear the resurrection story framed as the world's greatest love story. Digital platforms feature video testimonies alongside succinct gospel presentations, offering accessible invitations to explore faith. In every invitation, the question remains: "Do you want to live?"—prompting seekers to consider the hope that overcomes death's dominion.

9.7.2 Mobilizing Ordinary Believers for the Final Harvest

Jesus' lament in Luke 10:2—"the harvest is plentiful, but the laborers are few"—calls every Christian into participation. Prayer mobilization campaigns, such as "Pray 4 Harvest," focus corporate intercession on unreached peoples and local communities. Small-group "harvest hubs" train members in relational evangelism, equipping them with conversational tools and Gospel fluency. Digital mission strategies—social media challenges, livestreamed Q&A sessions, interactive apps—engage tech-savvy demographics with resurrection narratives. Churches track metrics not simply by attendance but by engagement: number of gospel conversations, follow-up appointments, and new believers discipled. This mobilization transforms passive congregants into empowered witnesses, advancing Easter's reign one person at a time. As ordinary believers engage the final harvest, they become instruments of the risen Christ's unstoppable momentum toward global renewal.

9.7.3 New Creation Languages: Art, Culture, and Innovation

Resurrection hope finds resonance in artistic expression that bridges sacred themes with contemporary culture. Visual artists create murals depicting the empty tomb in urban neighborhoods, offering public testimony to passersby. Musicians compose modern hymns that retell Easter's narrative in local musical idioms, while filmmakers produce short films that dramatize resurrection encounters. Storytelling evenings—featuring poetry, drama, and spoken word—invite artists to explore resurrection motifs in culturally relevant ways. Innovation labs within churches experiment with virtual reality "walk-in-the-tomb" experiences, enabling participants to step into Gospel scenes. By engaging art and culture, the church communicates Easter's power beyond traditional venues, reaching audiences that crave aesthetic and experiential dialogue. This creative evangelism demonstrates that resurrection hope transcends language barriers, speaking through beauty to hearts in every generation.

9.8 Community of Firstfruits: Corporate Hope

9.8.1 Communion of Saints in Resurrection Fellowship

Hebrews 12:1 envisions a "great cloud of witnesses" encircling believers—those heroes of faith who lived by resurrection promise. This communion of saints transcends temporal and geographic boundaries, uniting living and departed in the shared hope of Christ's return. Churches celebrate this fellowship through Heritage Sundays or All Saints' observances, recounting testimonies of past faithful who exemplified resurrection trust. Pilgrimages to historical Christian sites reinforce the tangible continuity of faith across ages. Small groups exchange stories of ancestors and mentors, building corporate identity rooted in resurrection perseverance. This fellowship enriches the church's self-understanding as firstfruits, encouraging each generation to contribute its own witness to the ongoing narrative of God's redemptive work.

9.8.2 Spiritual Gifts in Light of Eternity

Ephesians 4 depicts spiritual gifts as essential for building up the Body of Christ until all attain unity and maturity. In the context of eventual resurrection, these gifts take on eternal significance: speaking in tongues and prophecy offer glimpses of heavenly worship (Revelation 7:9–10), while teaching and pastoring prepare saints for eternal service. Churches integrate gift identification with eschatological teaching, helping members see their talents as investments in never-ending kingdom work. Worship services frequently include gift activation segments—encouraging participants to step out in faith, knowing that their service echoes into eternity. This perspective liberates believers from time-bound performance metrics, inviting them to trust that every act of service contributes to the everlasting harvest.

9.8.3 Ecumenical Dimension of Resurrection Unity

The resurrection confession unites Christians across denominational lines. Historic creeds—the Apostles' and

Nicene Creeds—proclaim a single resurrection event as the linchpin of faith. Ecumenical gatherings for Easter sunrise services and joint vigils exemplify this unity in practice. Collaborative mission initiatives, such as combined relief efforts in disaster zones, demonstrate resurrection reconciliation transcending doctrinal divisions. Theologians and pastors engage in dialogue around firstfruits and final consummation, seeking common ground in shared hope. By standing together on the reality of Easter morning, diverse communities model the reconciled kingdom, offering a powerful witness to a fragmented world. This ecumenical dimension of resurrection unity anticipates the time when every tribe and tongue will worship before the Lamb in harmony.

9.8.4 New Creation Fellowship Beyond Walls

Firstfruits fellowship extends beyond the sanctuary into neighborhoods, workplaces, and digital spaces. Community gardens, hosted by churches, embody new creation principles—sharing produce, teaching children, and stewarding land. Marketplace fellowships gather professionals for prayer and mutual encouragement, knitting resurrection community among peers. Online platforms—including virtual small groups and prayer networks—create unexpected connections across continents, manifesting cosmic reconciliation. These gatherings, though diverse in form, share a heartbeat: to embody resurrection fellowship wherever life unfolds. Through creative initiatives, the church breaks the barriers of geography and culture, sowing firstfruits communities that reflect the coming New Jerusalem in miniature.

Conclusion From the firstfruits offering at Sinai to the empty tomb at Golgotha and the new heavens and earth envisioned in Revelation, the biblical storyline arcs toward God's ultimate restoration of all things. Christ's resurrection inaugurates this grand narrative, guaranteeing human bodies will one day partake in imperishable life and promising cosmic renewal that will free creation from decay. In the interim, believers navigate the "already-but-not-yet" tension, living as firstfruits communities that embody kingdom values, share resurrection hope, and work toward justice, mercy, and restoration. Whether through sacramental previews, Spirit-empowered witness, compassionate outreach, or forward-looking worship, the church stands as the vanguard of God's new age, called to reveal glimpses of consummation amid present realities. As we await Christ's return, we do so with unwavering confidence that what God has begun in resurrection power will be brought to completion on the last day. May this vision of firstfruits to final fulfillment anchor our hope, guide our lives, and propel our mission, as we live and labor for the Day when the glory of the Lord shall cover the earth as the waters cover the sea.

Chapter 10: Proclaiming "He Has Risen Indeed!"

Proclaiming "He has risen indeed!" lies at the heart of Christian witness, shaping both our message and our methods. From the earliest apostles preaching in Jerusalem to modern digital evangelism, the church's highest aim has been to herald the reality of the empty tomb. This climactic truth has animated liturgies, inspired martyrs, fueled global missions, and permeated every cultural context in which the gospel has taken root. As we survey the manifold ways Easter has been proclaimed—through preaching, confession, song, symbol, testimony, and innovation—we will discover patterns and principles that remain vital today. Our goal is not merely to understand historical forms of proclamation, but to equip the contemporary church to incarnate Easter hope in ever-creative and contextually relevant ways. Ultimately, each method of proclamation, whether ancient or cutting-edge, centers on a unified purpose: to call humanity to encounter the living Christ, whose resurrection changes hearts, communities, and ultimately, the world.

10.1 Apostolic Foundations of Easter Proclamation

10.1.1 Apostolic Preaching in Jerusalem

On the day of Pentecost, Peter stood before a crowd in Jerusalem, filled with boldness by the Holy Spirit, and declared Jesus' death and resurrection as fulfillment of Scripture. Drawing on Joel's prophecy (Joel 2:28–29) and quoting Psalm 16, he testified that God had raised Jesus, whom they crucified, making Him both Lord and Christ (Acts 2:32–36). This inaugural Easter sermon led three thousand people to repentance and baptism (Acts 2:41), demonstrating the power of testimony grounded in resurrection fact. Stephen, in his speech before the Sanhedrin, wove resurrection themes into his defense, asserting that the temple's destruction and Israel's unfaithfulness pointed toward the risen Messiah's vindication (Acts 7:51–53). Paul, when addressing philosophers on Mars Hill, contextualized Easter proclamation by referencing the "unknown god" and declaring the God "who gives life to the dead and calls into existence the things that do not exist" (Acts 17:24–25, 31). In each case, apostolic preaching was anchored in historical claims backed by eyewitness testimony (1 Corinthians 15:6) and rooted in Old Testament expectation. Their model teaches that proclaiming "He has risen indeed!" demands contextual sensitivity, scriptural grounding, and Spirit-empowered boldness.

10.1.2 Creeds, Confessions, and Early Church Fathers

The earliest Christian preachers distilled the resurrection message into concise creedal formulas for catechesis and communal identity. The kernel of the kerygma appears in Paul's reference to what "I received" in 1 Corinthians 15:3–5—Christ died for our sins, was buried, and was raised on the third day—indicating that these truths circulated orally before being written. By the second century, the Apostles' Creed emerged, opening with "I believe in Jesus Christ... who was crucified, died, and was buried; He descended into hell; on the third day He rose again." Justin Martyr, in his First Apology, affirmed that the creeds were memorized by new believers and recited weekly (ca. 155 AD). Irenaeus, in Against

Heresies, expounded resurrection to counter Gnostic denials of the body, emphasizing that the physical rising of Christ secures believers' own bodily future. Augustine reflected similarly, linking sacramental participation to the creeds' confession and underscoring that Easter proclamation and baptism are inseparable. These early figures demonstrate that robust confessions and creeds ground proclamation in communal orthodoxy, equipping the church to safeguard truth even amid heretical challenges.

10.1.3 Martyrdom as Proclamation

Martyr narratives stand as some of the most potent Easter sermons, for they dramatize living and dying in the light of resurrection certainty. Polycarp of Smyrna, before being burned at the stake around 155 AD, famously proclaimed before the flames: "He has appeared, He has appeared, the Son of God appeared" (Martyrdom of Polycarp 14). His calm demeanor under execution testified more powerfully than any words could. Perpetua and Felicitas, catechumens martyred in Carthage (ca. 203 AD), clothed their deaths in resurrection imagery, viewing the arena as a path to immediate fellowship with Christ. Their martyr acts circulated widely, inspiring communal courage and underscoring the conviction that death gives way to life. Tertullian later reflected that the blood of martyrs became the seed of the church, demonstrating that sacrificial witness embodies the Easter proclamation most vividly. Martyrdom reminds the church that authentic proclamation sometimes demands the highest cost and that such costliest witness often lends the greatest credibility.

10.2 Liturgical Expressions of Easter Joy

10.2.1 The Easter Vigil and Paschal Liturgy

The Easter Vigil, observed on the night before Easter Sunday, constitutes the pinnacle of the Christian liturgical year. Beginning in darkness, worshipers gather to light the Paschal candle, symbolizing Christ as the Light of the World (John 8:12). The Exsultet, an ancient hymn, proclaims God's saving deeds from Creation through Exodus to resurrection, exulting, "O happy fault... by which we have been redeemed!" Scripture readings trace salvation history, culminating in the Easter proclamation: "Christ yesterday and today, the Beginning and the End" (Revelation 1:17–18). Baptismal rites follow, as catechumens are immersed and receive new life in Christ, reflecting Romans 6:4's burial and rising. The service moves toward the first celebration of the Eucharist, offering the risen Lord's body and blood in communion. This Paschal liturgy, rich in symbol and proclamation, invites participants not merely to remember Easter but to inhabit its reality, bridging worship and sacrament in proclaiming "He has risen indeed!"

10.2.2 Hymns and Canticles of Resurrection

Music has long been a vehicle for Easter proclamation, fusing doctrine with devotion. The ancient Latin hymn "Christians, to the Paschal Victim" (Victimae Paschali Laudes) invites the faithful to join Mary and the apostles in responding to the empty tomb. The Exsultet's soaring verses enthrall congregations with cosmic praise. During the medieval period, chorales such as "Christ ist erstanden" in German and Latin plainsong surged in Easter celebration, while the Reformation saw the birth of "Christ the Lord Is Risen Today" by Charles Wesley, whose joyful stanzas echo Matthew 28:6. In the modern era, worship songs like "Glorious Day (Living He Loved Me)" and "Forever (We Sing Hallelujah)" reiterate central resurrection truths in contemporary idioms. Canticles such as the Gloria and Te Deum frequently resurface in Easter liturgies, affirming the Lord's triumph with doxological fervor. Across centuries, these hymns and canticles have shaped the church's identity, embedding the Easter message in memory, song, and collective joy.

10.2.3 Visual Symbols and Sacred Space

Easter transforms sacred spaces through use of color, light, and imagery that communicate resurrection power visually. Liturgical fabrics shift from penitential purple to jubilant white and gold, while churches bloom with lilies—symbols of new life and purity. Stained glass windows depicting Christ's upward motion, the empty tomb, and the three Marys serve as catechetical art, teaching passersby the Easter story. Icons in Eastern traditions portray the Resurrection with Christ trampling down death's gates and raising Adam and Eve—an image known as the Harrowing of Hell—echoing 1 Peter 3:19's proclamation to spirits in prison. Processional banners emblazoned with rising suns and crosses guide worshipers in outdoor dawn services, visually proclaiming that light has overcome darkness. Even the placement of altar candles and Easter fire provides sensory testimony to the truth that the tomb is empty. Through these symbols, the church proclaims without words that death's power has been broken.

10.3 Personal Testimony and Relational Evangelism

10.3.1 The Power of First-Person Witness

Nothing resonates more deeply than a firsthand account of encountering the risen Christ. The apostle John records that Jesus appeared to "seven in Galilee" (John 21:1–14) and to more than five hundred at once (1 Corinthians 15:6), urging each to bear personal witness. In modern settings, individuals share stories of addiction overcome, depression lifted, or relationships restored through resurrection hope. Structuring such testimonies involves narrating life "before," describing the moment of encountering Christ—through Scripture, prayer, or community—and recounting life "after," marked by transformation and new purpose. Small-group environments, such as home fellowships, provide safe spaces for sharing these stories, reinforcing community bonds and inviting reciprocal vulnerability. Training in "Resurrection Testimony 101" equips believers to craft clear, concise, and gut-level narratives, ensuring that the proclamation "He has risen indeed!" is not abstract but incarnational.

10.3.2 Everyday Proclamation in Word and Deed

Proclaiming Easter extends beyond formal events into daily life. Christians have the opportunity at coffee shops, offices, and social gatherings to weave the resurrection message into casual conversation—perhaps by sharing how a difficult season was sustained by hope in Christ's victory over death (Romans 8:37–39). Acts of service—delivering meals, visiting shut-ins, advocating for justice—function as nonverbal sermons, embodying Matthew 25:35–36's call to care for "the least of these." When neighbors ask why believers sacrifice convenience to serve, this opens doors for sharing "He has risen indeed!" as the impulse behind compassion. Discipleship triads can include training in identifying such "divine appointments," empowering laypeople to seize everyday moments without feeling pressured into slick proselytism. In this way, the gospel permeates ordinary contexts, making resurrection hope tangible in word and deed.

10.3.3 Digital Storytelling and Relational Networks

The rise of digital platforms creates new venues for relational evangelism. Short video testimonies posted on Instagram or YouTube—under two minutes, with subtitles—can reach audiences far beyond one's physical neighborhood. Podcasts featuring interviews with individuals reflecting on how Easter hope sustained their families through crisis provide intimate spaces for deep connection. Virtual "Emmaus Road" small groups—gathered via Zoom or other meeting apps—allow participants to read Luke 24 together, share experiences of "burning hearts," and spur one another to proclaim resurrection truth. Facebook Live sessions enable impromptu Q&A about the significance of the empty tomb. Twitter threads can unpack resurrection themes in bite-sized reflections. By leveraging relational networks online, believers extend the "He has risen indeed!" proclamation into digital communities, building bridges and fostering spiritual encounters across geographical boundaries.

10.4 Media, Technology, and Global Broadcast

10.4.1 Radio, Television, and Streaming Easter Services

Radio ministries like the BBC's "Thought for the Day" and major Christian broadcasters have long syndicated Easter sermons, making resurrection proclamation accessible to listeners nationwide. Television networks air live Easter sunrise services from iconic venues—St. Peter's Basilica's Urbi et Orbi blessing, the Washington National Cathedral's festival service—projecting the Christian message into millions of homes. Churches now stream services on platforms like YouTube and Facebook Live, enabling viewers worldwide to join in real time, chat in prayer rooms, and receive virtual communion through guided ritual. On-demand archives offer Easter messages for listeners in disparate time zones, while podcasts ensure that the central Easter sermon can be downloaded and replayed. These media channels multiply the Easter witness exponentially, fulfilling Acts 1:8's call to be witnesses "to the end of the earth."

10.4.2 Social Media Campaigns and Hashtag Theology

In the digital era, hashtags have become rallying points for viral proclamation. Campaigns like #HeIsRisen, #EasterHope, and #ResurrectionSunday unify global conversations around shared content—images of sunrise services, brief devotionals, and low-fi testimonies. Instagram reels dramatizing the Gospel's resurrection narratives—using trending audio, creative visuals, and brief reflective voiceovers—can go viral, reaching viewers who might never darken a church door. Twitter threads by pastors unpack Easter themes in concise, tweet-sized insights, often linked to sermon recordings. Churches mobilize congregants to post sunrise photos with personal reflections, creating a mosaic of testimonies across time zones. Such hashtag theology harnesses networks of friends and followers, shifting Easter proclamation from the pulpit to the palm of every hand.

10.4.3 Film, Documentary, and Virtual Reality

Feature films such as "Risen" and "The Passion of the Christ" dramatize resurrection and crucifixion narratives for wide audiences, inviting both believers and skeptics into cinematic engagement with the Easter story. Documentaries like "The Case for Christ" present investigative accounts supporting historical resurrection claims, appealing to evidence-focused viewers. Virtual reality experiences—such as immersive "Walk through Jerusalem" apps—allow users to step into Gospel scenes: standing in the Garden Tomb, hearing Mary's "Woman, why are you weeping?" (John 20:15). Mobile apps offer guided 360-degree tours of Holy Week events, combining scripture, narration, and interactive reflection. These technological innovations demonstrate that Easter proclamation can embrace the cutting edge, offering embodied, experiential encounters with the risen Lord suited to the 21st century.

10.5 Cultural and Artistic Engagement

10.5.1 Drama, Pageants, and Easter Pageantry

Community Easter pageants invite both believers and non-believers to witness live reenactments of the Passion and Resurrection. Churches recruit local actors, stage realistic sets, and hold open-air performances in city squares, drawing crowds and offering free admission. Theater workshops help participants contextualize Gospel narratives in modern settings—subway stations, inner-city neighborhoods—bringing "He has risen indeed!" into familiar environments. Street dramas and flash mobs—where a procession suddenly gathers, Gospel excerpts are read, and a short skit enacts Mary's discovery of the empty tomb—surprise bystanders and spark conversations. These pageantries transform public space into a pulpit, using art to break down barriers of indifference or hostility.

10.5.2 Visual Arts, Murals, and Street Installations

Visual artists commissioned by churches or community coalitions create murals that depict sunrise over Golgotha, the angel rolling back the stone, and Christ's triumphant emergence. Pop-up exhibits in urban alleys showcase paintings on plywood or fabric, accompanied by QR codes linking to brief Gospel explanations. Street installations—sculptures of broken chains or an open door motif—symbolize resurrection liberation in public parks. Graffiti festivals invite local youth to spray-paint resurrection verses in central plazas, under graffiti-artist mentorship that upholds both artistic integrity and theological depth. Such public art normalizes Easter proclamation, making resurrection imagery part of everyday visual culture.

10.5.3 Music Festivals and Concerts

Ecumenical Easter concerts gather choirs, orchestras, and contemporary bands to proclaim resurrection through music. Churches collaborate with community centers to host "Resurrection Music Festivals," blending classical works such as Handel's *Messiah* with modern worship sets. Gospel choirs, jazz ensembles, and multicultural dance troupes showcase the diversity of Easter praise, inviting audiences to experience resurrection joy through performance. Improvisational worship sessions—led by musicians and spoken-word artists—allow spontaneous Easter expressions, reflecting 1 Corinthians 14:15's call to worship "with the Spirit." Music festivals become both evangelistic outreach and celebratory proclamation, echoing Psalm 98:4: "Make a joyful noise to the Lord, all the earth; break forth into jubilant song and sing praises!"

10.6 Global Mission and Festal Witness

10.6.1 Cross-Cultural Easter Celebrations

Across the globe, indigenous churches contextualize Easter in local customs. In Ghana, sunrise services on hills combine traditional drumming with Gospel preaching. In India, Passion plays reenacted in regional languages draw on folk theatre conventions, making resurrection narrative accessible. Latin American barrio churches integrate Easter proclamation with community feasts and street processions, blending Catholic and Evangelical elements. These cross-cultural celebrations demonstrate that "He has risen indeed!" transcends cultural boundaries, speaking in the idioms of diverse peoples. Missionaries partnering with local leaders learn to embed theological clarity in culturally resonant forms, ensuring that proclamation is both faithful and fruitful.

10.6.2 Interfaith and Public Square Engagement

Easter egg hunts in public parks, sponsored by church coalitions, open opportunities for relational evangelism among secular families. Sunrise breakfast gatherings—often hosted by civic leaders in town squares—foster goodwill and shared reflection on life's meaning. Interfaith dialogues around the theme "Life Triumphs over Death" bring together Christian, Jewish, Muslim, and secular thinkers to discuss universal hopes and points of tension, fostering mutual respect even amid disagreement. Civic partnerships for charitable events— free medical camps, community cleanups—conducted on Easter weekend, demonstrate resurrection compassion in action and invite media coverage. Such public square engagements ensure that the Christian proclamation resonates beyond church walls, witnessing to the common yearnings for hope and renewal.

10.6.3 Digital Mission Conferences and Webinars

Virtual mission summits—featuring keynote addresses, breakout sessions, and digital prayer rooms—equip global participants to strategize Easter proclamation in their contexts. Webinars on contextualization, media use, and digital storytelling share best practices, from producing short-form Easter devotionals to running social media ad campaigns targeted at unchurched demographics. Online "Easter Bootcamps" train believers in relational evangelism, testimony sharing, and hosting virtual prayer gatherings. These digital gatherings transcend borders, enabling missionaries in remote areas to access cutting-edge methods and collaborate with peers. By harnessing the internet as mission field, the church multiplies its Easter witness, ensuring that "He has risen indeed!" echoes in every language and platform.

10.7 Sustaining the Proclamation in the Local Church

10.7.1 Year-Round "He Has Risen Indeed" Culture

To avoid Easter as a once-a-year event, churches embed resurrection language into weekend services, small groups, and youth programs throughout the calendar. A quarterly "Resurrection Sunday" can remind congregations to refocus on Easter themes amid other liturgical seasons. Devotional booklets—published monthly—carry Easter reflections, tying Pentecost back to resurrection life. Sermon series like "Resurrection and..." (Work, Relationships, Justice) sustain thematic continuity. Youth retreats titled "Resurrection Retreat" anchor adolescent discipleship in Easter hope. By normalizing resurrection emphasis year-round, churches cultivate a culture in which "He has risen indeed!" becomes the lens for every ministry, sustaining momentum beyond the annual celebration.

10.7.2 Equipping Leaders and Lay Ministers

Effective proclamation requires intentional training. Workshops on crafting compelling resurrection sermons help pastors and lay preachers sharpen their kerygmatic focus. Testimony-writing seminars guide laypeople in articulating personal resurrection encounters with clarity and impact. Media-production clinics teach volunteers to record, edit, and promote Easter videos on multiple platforms. Resource libraries—comprised of graphics, liturgies, sermon outlines, and children's materials—equip ministry teams to plan creative Easter events. Cross-training sessions deepen collaboration among worship, communications, and outreach teams, ensuring integrated proclamation. By investing in equipping, churches multiply their capacity to proclaim "He has risen indeed!" with excellence and consistency.

10.7.3 Renewal Movements and Easter Revivals

Periodic "Easter Revival" weekends invite guest speakers, extended worship, and corporate baptism to recapture the passion of Easter's early days. Homecoming services encourage former members to re-engage, symbolically returning to the empty tomb. City-wide prayer walks—stemming from Acts 1's Jerusalem waiting—invoke the risen Lord's blessing on neighborhoods. Annual "Resurrection Conferences" gather multiple congregations for combined worship and training. These renewal movements spark fresh evangelistic energy, replenish spiritual fervor, and reaffirm communal commitment to proclaim Easter truth. By hosting revival-style events, churches tap into a long tradition of Pentecostal renewal that underscores the ongoing relevance of "He has risen indeed!"

10.8 Overcoming Obstacles to Easter Proclamation

10.8.1 Secular Skepticism and Scientific Objections

In a scientifically oriented culture, skepticism about miracle claims can stifle Easter proclamation. Addressing these doubts requires respectful dialogue and evidence-based reasoning. Archaeological findings—such as ossuaries bearing names mentioned in New Testament narratives—and textual studies reinforcing manuscript reliability bolster the case for historical resurrection. Philosophical arguments for God's existence and discussions of the coherence of miracles provide intellectual frameworks. Simultaneously, personal testimonies of spiritual and emotional transformation offer experiential counters. Ministries like "Science & Faith" conferences create spaces where scientists and theologians model gracious engagement. Equipping leaders to navigate such conversations ensures that "He has risen indeed!" resonates not only emotionally but rationally as well.

10.8.2 Religious Pluralism and Cultural Resistance

In pluralistic societies, overtly Christian messages can be met with suspicion or indifference. Contextualizing Easter proclamation entails translating key terms—resurrection, salvation, new life—into culturally resonant language while retaining theological integrity. Interfaith forums offer opportunities to identify shared longings—justice, hope, peace—without diluting distinctives. Compassion initiatives—hunger relief, free clinics—demonstrate resurrection love in action, opening doors for deeper conversations. Storytelling approaches honor listeners' backgrounds, inviting them into dialogue rather than delivering monologues. Training in cultural intelligence and sensitivity prevents missteps and fosters authentic relationships. Through patient, contextualized engagement, the proclamation "He has risen indeed!" can transcend cultural barriers.

10.8.3 Burnout and Disillusionment in Ministry

Year after year of orchestrating Easter events can wear down even the most dedicated ministers. To sustain zeal, churches provide rest rhythms—Sabbath sabbaticals after Easter peak seasons and peer support groups for debriefing. Celebrating small victories—new lives touched, testimonies shared—rekindles passion. Pastors model vulnerability by sharing their own cracks and restorations, echoing Peter's restoration by Christ (John 21:15–19). Spiritual retreats focused on personal encounter with the risen Lord replenish inner resources. Accountability partnerships help leaders maintain healthy boundaries and realistic expectations. When resurrection proclamation becomes life-giving rather than merely task-driven, ministers move from burnout to empowered endurance.

Conclusion Proclaiming "He has risen indeed!" has taken myriad forms across two millennia—from Peter's first Pentecost sermon amid Jerusalem's crowds to virtual reality experiences 2,000 years later. Yet whether through the spoken word, the sung hymn, the dancer's leap, the artist's brushstroke, or the web-streamed service, the goal remains unchanged: to call humanity into encounter with the living Christ. The historic foundations of apostolic preaching and creedal confession equip us with time-tested content; the sacramental and liturgical traditions embed Easter truth in communal life; the power of personal testimony and relational networks ensures dynamic engagement; and the innovations of media, art, and technology open fresh horizons for global mission. As we navigate secular skepticism, cultural pluralism, and ministry fatigue, our confidence rests in the empty tomb that proclaims death's defeat. May every generation, every congregation, and every believer find renewed inspiration to echo across the ages: He has risen indeed!

www.ingramcontent.com/pod-product-compliance
Lightning Source LLC
Chambersburg PA
CBHW060321050426
42449CB00011B/2596